Montreux Riviera
Switzerland

Farrol Kahn

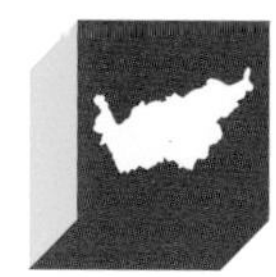

Farrol Kahn

Farrol Kahn is a journalist and author of travel books. He lives in Switzerland and knows the region well. Montreux Riviera is his third book on the country. The others include the Valais, the undiscovered canton and the ski and golf resort, Crans Montana which has the cleanest air in Switzerland. His local knowledge ensures a memorable holiday.

Published by Valais Books
Avenue de Corsier 16
CH-1800 Vevey
Switzerland

Printed by Gutenberg Press Ltd.
Gudja Road
Tarxien
Malta GXQ 2902

Design and layout: AZZZA Limited, UK

ISBN 978-3-9524208-2-9

The book will have a website link www.montreuxriviera.me to whet the appetite for visiting the region.
It has been created by Graham Rivers, a web designer. (www.grageo.co.uk).

Books on the Valais-The Undiscovered Swiss Canton, Crans-Montana-The Ski and Golf Resort and the Montreux Riviera are available from the Swiss publisher:

Tel: +41(0)27 934 1721
Mob +41(0) 79 421 8981
Email: farrol.kahn@bluewin.ch

To Myriam and her parents, Robert and Maryse Roy

Acknowledgements

The author would like to thank the many people in the Montreux Riviera whom he interviewed and assisted him during the course of writing the book. In particular, Dr Dirk Craen who immediately provided a list of the movers and shakers in the region; the mayors who are over-the-top busy such as Laurent Wehrli, Laurent Ballif, Lyonel Kaufman, Patricia Dominique Lachat and Jacques Andre Conne as well as Christoph Sturny of the Montreux-Vevey Tourism. The pioneer families: Josephine Christidis-Mayer, her husband Petros Christidis and children Alexandre and Stephanie; Monique Touzeau, her husband Maurice and children Beatrice and Bruno; Anne Rapin-Zurcher and her mother Anoinette Zurcher; Toni and Barbara Mittermair; François Margot; Anne-Christine Meylan; Shahriar Gharibi; Anne-Marie and Neil Harwood and Grainne and Jean-Louis Dubler; Bernadette and Rolf Messmer and David and Laurence Tarnowski. The hospitality and business sector: Michael Smithuis; Andrés Oppenheim; Rémy Crégut; Ezio Vialmin; Jerome Ake; Jean-Claude Biver and Matthieu Naef; Goldenpass and Chillon Castle; Also in gratitude: Abrezol, Pierre; Abundo, Nicolas; Aebischer, Patrick; Aellen, Fabienne; Aguet, Pierre; Amsallem, Thierry; Baumann, Gerard; Beldi, Luc; Beuchat, Nicole; Bise, Pierre; Bornand, Roger; Boutilly, Jean-Marc; Brunet Hélène; Budry, Christian; Buri, Laurent; Clivaz, Grégoire; Coutaz, Sylvia; de Vries, Jean-Christophe; De Crousaz, Francois; Delessert, Philippe; Dorta, Gaudenz; Dos Santos, Marta; Ducrot, Patrice; du Marchie van Voorthuysen, Nicole and Paul; Durgnat, Fabienne; Elöd, Bernadette; Ferla, Michel; Ferrari, Olivier; Frund, Benoît; Furrer, Grégoire; Gademann, Bernhard; Morgan, Charles; Gauer, Jay; Jean-Jacques Gauer; Geiser, Thomas; Hausmann, Grégoire; Hausmann, Ywan; Heini, Dr Adrian; Hennessy, Clive; Hou, Judy; Jaton, Mathieu; Joye, Sandra; Julliard, Julie Enckell; Kamerzin, Mireille; Keller, Pierre; Knight, Christine; Kohli, Doriane;Leder Alain; Lepre, Luciano and Verena; Locher, André;Longet-Voruz, Patricia; Marthaler, Laurent; Mayer, Estelle; Meillet, Gilles; Merali, Naseem; Meylan,Lionel; Michel, François; Ming, Christophe and Nicolas; Moser, Patrick; Moutarlier, Lucien; Muller, Norbert; Pastori, Pierre; Perroud, Pierre-Alain; Pfeifer, Prof Dr Andrea; Pfiffner, Albert; Prénat, Anne-Caroline; Rion, Maude; Rondez, Florent; Saurais, Catherine; Schenk, François; Sommer, Gisele; Steinmann, Vincent; Tavassoli, Reza; Vlad, Ilinca; von Siebenthal, Claudia; Yudochkina, Natalia; Zeller, Ursula.

Lastly, a special thanks to AZZZA, Paul Bizzell and Anita Zabilevska, a talented graphic designer and veteran of my three books. It is a pleasure to work with her and I admire her magical skill in creating page layouts even after my many changes.

Photo Credits: There are numerous sources for the photos including my own. Thanks again to John Cosford who now has assisted me with three books and Myriam with this, her first. Other credits include: Montreux-Riviera Tourism; Stéphane Le Nédic for the map; Ban Ki-moon & Laurent Wehrli © Sieber; Dr Dirk Craen, © Lionel Flusin; Quincy Jones, Mathieu Jaton, © Philippe Dutoit; Thierry Amsallem and 'Claude Nobs private collection.'; Antoinette Zurcher, Anne Rapin-Zurcher; dungeon © Chateau Chillon; Confiserie Zurcher; Victoria Hotel; Grand Hotel Suisse Majestic; Fairmont Le Montreux Palace; Estelle Mayer © Patrick Martin 24/heures; Le Palais Orientale; European University Business School; Paul and Nicole Le Liboson; Clinique La Prairie; Montreux Noel; Goldenpass; Oron castle © Swisscastles; © glacier 3000; Pierre Bise; Montreux-Vevey Tourism © Christof Sonderegger; Laurent Ballif; Pierre Abrezol; Jenisch Museum; Le Corbusier Villa "Le Lac"; Confrérie des Vignerons Museum; Jerome Ake © Edouard Curchod; Major Davel; Cully Classique © Anne-Laure Lechat; Tour de Peilz © Christophe Karlen; Nestlé Historical Archives Nestlé, Vevey; Philippe DuToit MJ & QJ; David Tarnowski, Tarnowski dishes José Crespo copyright; Roman Mayer © Chantal Dervey/24heures and Siegfried von Känel © Nestec S.A., Vevey.

Contents

Introduction

The Montreux Riviera Tourist region comprises 17 communes extending from Lutry to Villeneuve and including parts of three districts:
District of Lavaux-Oron: Bourg-en-Lavaux, Lutry, Puidoux, Chexbres, Rivaz, St-Saphorin.
District of Riviera-Pays d'Enhaut: Chardonne, Corseaux, Jongny, Corsier, Vevey, St-Légier, Blonay, la Tour-de-Peilz, Montreux, Veytaux.
District of Aigle: Villeneuve.

Free transport and 50% reduction on tickets

A big bonus of visiting the region is the Montreux Rivera Card which offers tourists free public transport and 50% discount on boat trips, mountain railways and tickets to museums and amusement parks. The only condition is that you have to be a guest in a hotel, holiday apartment, stay in a camping site or be a client in a clinic.
See www.http:// files.gadmin.ch/24838?CFID=123905868&CFTOKEN=39867656 or http:// www.montreuxriviera.com/files/...

Interactive Benches

A new dimension has been added to holidays in Montreux Riviera. The resort has been renowned for attracting famous poets, writers, actors, musicians, artists and engineers, among others. Now tourists can meet the famous visitors during walks near 31 benches with personalised signposts. A short text on the signpost explains the link of the personality with the region. All they need to complete it - a smartphone to access the dedicated website or the application with which they scan the signpost that gives them access to multimedia content.

"The unique concept 'Rencontres & Inspiration' (Encounters & Inspiration) offers tourists the opportunity to follow in the footsteps of the many distinguished people that have been welcomed here," said Christoph Sturny, Director of Montreux-Vevey Tourism. "We have a very rich cultural heritage which tourists can encounter through stopping at the benches. They too can be inspired by the incredible panoramas, nature and creative work by coming here."

Imagine listening to an extract from One Trip Abroad by Scott Fitzgerald at the bench near the funicular station in Glion or to the Prisoner of Chillon by Lord Byron at the Quai Chatelanat, Veytaux. For French literature, you have a choice of Jean-Jacques Rousseau's Julie ou la Nouvelle Héloïse at Quai de Clarens, Victor Hugo's Le Rhin at Esplanade de St-Martin or Alphonse de Lamartine or Alphonse Daudet. For those who have penchant for royalty, they can learn more about Sissi, Empress Elizabeth of Austria who met a tragic death if they visit her statue at Avenue de Chillon 92, Territet or her bench in Caux.

In music, there is something for everyone from Pop (Freddie Mercury on Quai des Fleurs, Montreux) classical (Igor Stravinsky in Clarens, and Clara Haskil in Vevey) and jazz (Claude Nobs near the casino of Montreux). For the aficionados of art, you have Gustave Courbet at La Tour de Peilz; Hugo Pratt, Italian comic creator of Corto Maltese in Grandvaux and Ferdinand Hodler in Chexbres. The illustrious Brits include Graham Greene at Le Sentier, Chemin du Grand-Pin, Corseaux and the still ever popular Charlie Chaplin with his statue at Quai Perdonnet and his bench in Parc Chaplin, Corsier. The Russians are represented by their great writers, Leon Tolstoy at Quai de Vernex,Clarens; Fiodor Dosteyevsky at Chemin de l'Espérance, Vevey and Vladimir Nabokov in Caux. Even foreign politicians who were founding fathers of their countries such as Mahatma Gandhi in Villeneuve and Gustav Mannerheim in Glion sojourned at the resort.

Finally, among the 31 personalities, there is the famous architect, Le Corbusier at Villa "Le Lac", Route de Lavaux 21, Corseaux and the bench on Quai Ernest Ansermet in Vevey, the industrialist Henri Nestlé at Vevey and the authoress of Heidi, Johanna Spyri, at the Rue de la Gare 25, Montreux.

"There are several advantages of 'Rencontres & Inspiration'," said Christoph Sturny who is proud of the concept of interactive benches. "Tourists can combine exercise with culture, discover places off the beaten track and our heritage in a dynamic way."

A map with the list of all the famous guests is available at the six tourist information offices at Montreux, Vevey,Chexbres, Cully, Lutry and Villeneuve.

Website: www.rencontres-inspiration.com.

Illustration : fabriquedimages.ch

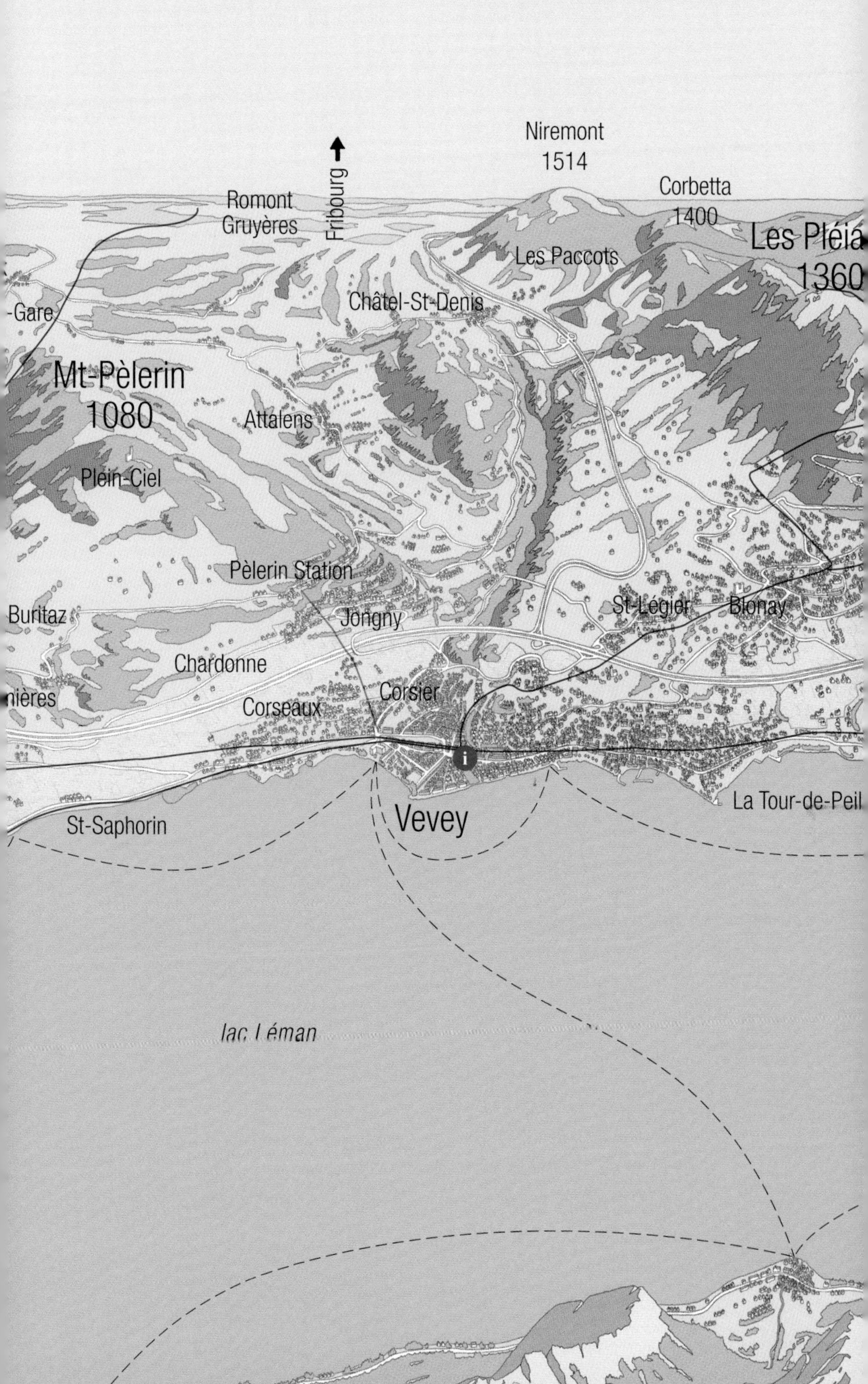
Niremont
1514
Fribourg
Romont
Gruyères
Corbetta
1400
Les Pléia
1360
Les Paccots
-Gare
Châtel-St-Denis
Mt-Pèlerin
1080
Attalens
Plein-Ciel
Pèlerin Station
St-Légier
Blonay
Buritaz
Jongny
Chardonne
Corsier
nières
Corseaux
La Tour-de-Peil
Vevey
St-Saphorin
lac Léman

Le Moléson
2002
Le Folly
1730
Niremont
1514
Fribourg
Corbetta
1400
Romont
Gruyères
Les Pléiades
1360
Les Paccots
Châtel-St-Denis
Les Tenasses
Vallon de V
Lally
Attalens
Pèlerin Station
Chamb
St-Légier
Blonay
Jongny
donne
Chailly
Corsier
Corseaux
La Tour-de-Peilz
Vevey
lac Léman

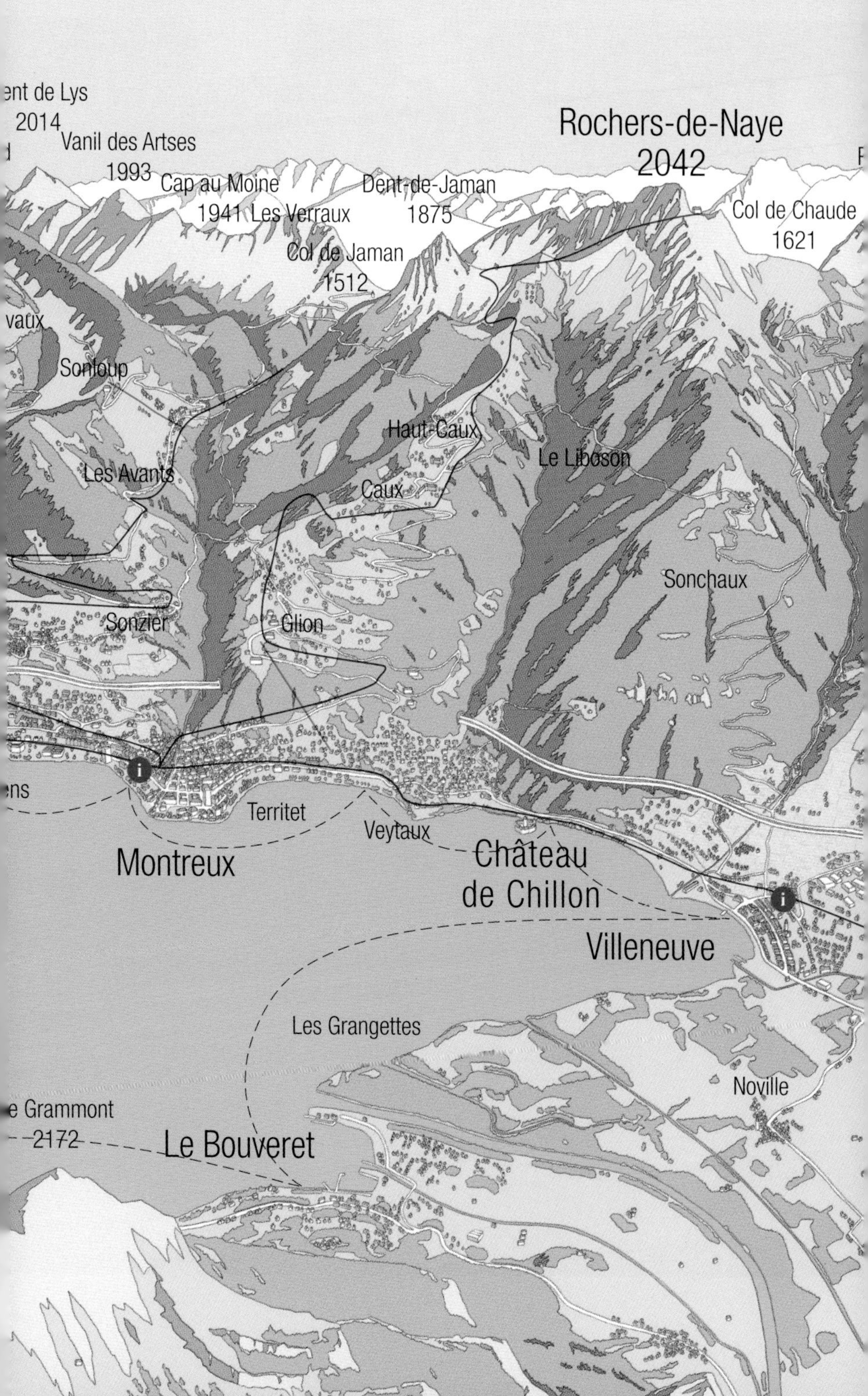
ent de Lys
2014
Vanil des Artses
1993
Cap au Moine
1941
Les Verraux
Dent-de-Jaman
1875
Col de Jaman
1512
Rochers-de-Naye
2042
Col de Chaude
1621
vaux
Sonloup
Les Avants
Haut-Caux
Caux
Le Liboson
Sonchaux
Sonzier
Glion
ens
Territet
Veytaux
Montreux
Château
de Chillon
Villeneuve
Les Grangettes
Noville
e Grammont
2172
Le Bouveret

Chapter 1. Montreux

History

Montreux with its microclimate, hot enough for fig and palm trees and with mild winters, has always attracted visitors from the crowned heads of Europe such as Sissi, Empress Elizabeth of Austria to artists, writers and musicians. Jean-Jaques Rousseau kickstarted the tourism with his books, Julie or the new Heloise (1761) which was a best seller with 70 editions before 1800 and Reveries of a solitary walker (1782). Lord Byron followed with The prisoner of Chillon (1816) and later visitors arrived in droves.

The first two hotels opened their doors in 1835 and until the First World War, the resort enjoyed a golden age. De rigueur was for families to come for stays of months' duration and they expected the hotels to provide varied entertainments. The Fairmont Montreux Palace with its 15 banqueting rooms offered guests ballroom dancing, bridge, a theatre, a billiard room, a shooting range, a skating and roller skating rink. The hotel together with the other Belle Epoch Suisse Majestic have been renovated and can still provide exceptional conference facilities together with the Miles Davis and Stravinsky auditoria.

Montreux has also been an inspiration for writers, artists and musicians. Hans Christian Andersen who suffered from bronchitis and came for treatment in Glion wrote the Ice Maiden and Ernest Hemingway on a visit wrote chapters from A Farewell to Arms. In Clarens, Tchaikovsky composed the Concerto for violin and Igor Stravinsky the Rite of Spring.

Oskar Kokoschka spent the last 25 years of his life in Villeneuve and to cap it all, Vladimir Nabokov lived with his wife Véra on the sixth floor of the Fairmont Montreux Palace hotel for 16 years until his death in 1977. During this period he was a prolific writer of novels, poetry, short stories, drama and works of criticism as well as his final autobiography, Speak Memory: An autobiography revisited. He was also a lepidopterist and his favourite hobby was butterfly hunting.

"It's only an accident that we're here," said Nabokov. "My wife was here in

1914 with her family and when we passed through here in the 1960s she said 'why not stay for a while' and we've been here ever since.'"

Montreux is the jewel of the Swiss Riviera which even outshines the resorts of Cannes and Nice. The treelined promenade on the lakeshore has flower displays throughout the year and is pedestrianized as there is no busy road to cross.

The town of Montreux until the 1960s consisted of 24 vineyard villages and was bounded by Clarens to the west, Territet to the east and Glion to the north.

People

The Mayor

Laurent Wehrli, the mayor of Montreux is into his first term of office and fourth as a member of the government of the city. He presides over the most international city in Switzerland with 148 nationalities. The appeal of the largest city on the Swiss Riviera is due to the microclimate, its beautiful location between the Alps and the lake, sports all year round and its key attractions of the Montreux Jazz festival and the Christmas market.

From left Ban Ki-moon, Secretary General UN, Laurent Wehrli, Mayor Montreux ©Sieber

"Montreux began as a winter resort," said Laurent Wehrli with a smile. "We put ice hockey on the map in Switzerland. The third congress of the International Ice Hockey Federation (Ligue International de Hockey sur Glace) was held in Montreux in 1910. But even before that we had two major promoters of the Swiss Riviera. There was Jean-Jacques Rousseau and Lord Byron. Soon tourists followed and grand hotels were built to accommodate them."

Wehrli has a MA in Literature from the university of Lausanne. He won the White House prize and spent a year in Kent State university where he carried out Nato studies. His speciality was World War II. Although, he was an editor of an economic review he has had extensive experience in local and cantonal politics. He also spent 15 years in tourism and is a member of the Swiss delegation to the Council of Europe for local and regional areas.

"What I learnt from my year in the US," he said, "is 'you can do it.' It encapsulates the Obama spirit. I've never had a mentor and as mayor, I act as a catalyst. I like to organise things and see them realised. A good example is the Stravinsky conference centre which is the new wing of the Montreux Music and Convention Centre. It is designed for events from 300 to 3,000 and is equipped with a high-tech auditorium. But you never can do it alone. Each stone which makes a wall is the work of a single man or woman. And the wall is the result of many."

Montreux has a population of over 26,000 of which some 48% are foreigners. The figure does not include the 2,600 international students who attend the schools in the area. There is a selection from hospitality management schools such as Glion and the Swiss Education Group in Caux and Montreux; the Monte Rosa boarding school and the European University Business school.

"We are essentially a welcome destination," he said. "As such we have beautiful Belle Epoque hotels, many Michelin & Gault Millau restaurants, renowned private clinics and famous schools of all sorts. The top three attractions are the climate, the landscape which was not amenable to agriculture and the fact that we are free of industrial chimneys. The big plus is that the Swiss Rivera stretches from Villeneuve with the Chillon Castle to the marvellous old town of Vevey and the UNESCO vineyards of Lavaux. It's an ideal place for holidays and conferences as we have much to offer in culture and entertainment. We even have a top casino in the resort. Visitors are spoilt for choice."

Sinjoor From Antwerp

"With his background, it's only natural that Dr Dirk Craen is a high flyer and an outstanding president of European University business school."

Dr Dirk Craen heads the European University business school which has four campuses in Montreux, Geneva, Munich and Barcelona. He is a businessman par excellence and prior to being president, he founded the business school in Montreux. Under his watch the European University has already risen to 34th place from 54th in the QS rankings of Global business schools. It is in the same list of 200 schools in which the renowned INSEAD, London Business School and Oxford University (Said Business School) are among the top.

"I established European University SA in Montreux in May 1985," he said, "because there is a pool of over 20,000 high school students in the lake Geneva area."

His achievement is even greater when you realise that he had been warned off as 14 finishing schools had closed in the area over the past 25 years. But Dirk Craen thrives on challenges. He is the kind of entrepreneur who could turn around an ailing company or come up with a new product line.

"I went to the Jesuit high school in Antwerp which is better known as de

Dr Dirk Craen, President, European University Business School ©Lionel Flusin

OLVC," he said, "and graduated from the European university in Antwerp with a MBA. I was fortunate in my internships because I visited the production lines of several top companies like Rolex and Oerlikon Bürhle. My father worked for a coated abrasive company SIA in Frauenfeld and therefore my love for Switzerland grew in those early days."

The European University is an international business school. The curriculum offered promotes managerial skills, business ethics and entrepreneurial initiatives vital to finding positions in the global business market. It is based on the American university model with top European management practices. The university encourages its students to explore their entrepreneurship without boundaries while pursuing their studies. Besides the usual international undergraduate and graduate degree programmes, it offers an innovative business foundation programme which prepares students for the challenges and knowledge of the bachelor's degrees.

"The key element of our courses is entrepreneurship and intrapreneurship - being an entrepreneur within a large corporation," he said. "To operate successfully globally, we encourage students to take direct responsibility for turning an idea into a profitable finished product through assertive risk-taking and innovation. My mentor was Professor Warren Bennis, a pioneer in leadership studies and advisor to four US presidents."

One of the first examples of intrapreneurship occurred at Apple computer. Steve Jobs said in an interview with Newsweek in 1985 that the Macintosh team was what was commonly known as intrapreneurship. "Only a few years before the term was coined - a group of people going, in essence, back to the garage, but in a large company." Other companies have also encouraged intrapreneurship like 3M, Intel and Google who allowed employees to spend up to 20% of their time pursuing their own projects.

"The first thing the new generation of undergraduates need is focus," said Dirk Craen. "They are weaned on iPads and on social networking sites. They appear not to have a clue of what a reputation is or how to converse or write an essay. You just have to look at their Face book sites and you'll discover the lack of discipline and lack of respect for society or a system. My philosophy is what I call the ABC of words and provides focus for the undergraduates. 'A' stands for achievements, action and anticipation. 'B' stands for be better and be bright. 'C' stands for be creative, be a changer, be curious, be confident and stick to a commitment. Our classes are small and we evaluate them on a daily basis with regard to their personality and work."

One of the unique features of the European University is Learning from Leaders programme whereby it invites distinguished guests as speakers. Among those are included Adolf Ogi, former president of Switzerland; Jean-Claude Biver, chairman of Hublot Watches; Patrick Maeseneire, CEO of Adecco; Marc Hayek, CEO Blancpain; Moritz Suter, founder of Crossair; Lu Yu Cheng, former Executive Vice Mayor of Beijing; Nayla Hayek, chairwoman of Swatch Group; R.Seetharaman, CEO of Doha Bank; Peter R. Vogt, Deputy Executive Vice-President of Nestlé and Head of HR & Centre Administration; Wendelin von Boch, CEO of Villeroy & Boch; and Yves Leterme, former Prime Minister of Belgium and Deputy Secretary-General of OECD.

"I often tell the story about the financial crisis and how it could be avoided," he said. "The people responsible were highly capable in the sense of technocrats. But they lacked social responsibility. Of course, all the business schools have since learnt and have introduced business ethics into their courses. From the start of European University 40 years ago, we put the human side into people."

The fact that Dirk Craen was born in Antwerp - he is a sinjoor (derived from the Spanish senor which means posh mr) is significant in his role as president. He has grown up in a city which is not only known as being tolerant but also as an international commercial centre. As far back as 1531, Antwerp established the world's first bourse or stock exchange for financial and commodity trading which predated shares. With his background, it's only natural that Dr Dirk Craen is a high flyer and an outstanding president of European University business school. In 2014, he was awarded the Order of the Crown (Belgium) by royal decree.

From left Quincy Jones, Mathieu Jaton ©Philippe Dutoit

Miracles Made Me

Most people who live in Montreux have been touched by Claude Nobs' genius at some time or other either through personal contact or by the festival. But none so much than by Mathieu Jaton who became his successor at the Montreux Jazz Festival.

"We had an intuitive relationship like father and son," said Mathieu Jaton, CEO of the MJF. "There were three occasions in my life which I would term miraculous. The first was when I was a teenager and started to play in a jazz rock band. It was styled on John McLaughlin electric Mahavishnu orchestra and Colosseum. My dream was to be heard by Claude who was a director of Warner records. So I rang him up and when I gave my name, he said,'I know who you are. You're the son of Philippe. We went to scouts together. Come and see me tomorrow.' I was bowled over by his response. What I hadn't realised was that he had grown up with my father. So the next day, he listened to our non- professional music and gave us advice."

Mathieu's family were keen on classical music and had a Steinway grand piano. Consequently, young talented competitors in the Clara Haskill International competition would stay at their home for two weeks. He remembered at the age of four slipping down at night sometimes to listen to the pianists practicing and falling asleep under the piano. Later, he would play LPs of Mozart and eventually graduated to Pink Floyd and Led Zeppelin.

He loved the riffs of Roger Waters and which pushed him to buy a Fender stratocaster electric guitar.

"The second occasion I connected with Claude was when I was doing extras at the Montreux Palace hotel," he said. "It was the night of the Spring Ball and I was working long hours. At 5 am, I was tapped on the shoulder and when I looked round it was Claude. He invited me to come to the chalet and meet the Monty Python creator and his wife. I could've easily refused as I was totally exhausted and clearing my last table. But I came because he said that he needed my help. The truth was that he could've managed on his own. But from then on Claude offered me extras at the festival."

Mathieu recalled his first Montreux Jazz Festival concert in the casino aged 12. Everything in his mind is still clear. B.B.King on the stage of the casino, the chairs, the audience. It was a wow! Like most young people in the Montreux Riviera, Mathieu was drawn to a career in hospitality and studied at the Lausanne Hospitality School. But when he gained his diploma in 1999, he had second thoughts.

"I realised that all my life I'd been more interested in organising stuff," he said. "Organising my friends' birthdays, Christmas and New Year parties. Organization was in my blood. I loved serving people. So I decided to call Claude the same day. The secretary told me that he was at a board meeting the entire day. During the afternoon, without knowing that I had called him, he rang me on an impulse and asked if I was interested in a marketing and sponsorship position. Or did I want to do something else. I said yes. It was August 15, 1999. I'll always remember the day until the end of my life. That was the third occasion. So we worked together for 15 years. There was 40 years difference in our ages."

Mathieu got accustomed to Claude's working habits. Sometimes he would say, "Tomorrow we're going to New York." And his young associate would reply, "Cool." But later there were a few occasions when Mathieu would disagree and Claude would accept that he was pushing the button too far.

Claude Disappeared

Two years later in 2001, he told Mathieu that he wanted him to come to the board meeting. It was an unusual request because the office was separate from the board.

"So I went along and was taking notes," he said, "when the chairman suddenly turned to me and told me that they had decided together with Claude to offer me the position of Secretary General. Later when we were driving along, I asked him what this meant? He told me he was 65 and had to think about the future. 'But I don't have the experience', I said. 'You can do things, I can't do,' he replied. 'Remember, I didn't hire you, I chose you.' The position fell upon my head. I was just under Claude in the management chart and responsible for marketing and sponsorship.12 years later when I acquired the entire information, Claude disappeared."

In 2013, Claude Nobbs died after an accident on Christmas Eve during a cross-country skiing trip. The 37 year-old Mathieu Jaton was elected unanimously by the board of trustees to become CEO of the Montreux Jazz Festival. The brand which had started as a means to attract tourists had achieved fame worldwide. In its heyday, the resort was known as the English Rivera until the Second World War. Montreal jazz festival was the largest in terms of attendance but Montreux was also one of the most famous.

"The world of music has changed a lot since the 1980s and 1990s," said Mathieu. "The recording companies were dominant and managed stars like Aretha Franklin and James Brown. But since 2000 when music was downloaded on the internet, the recording companies lost power. Nowadays, artists have to tour and play. They hate days off. Take the example of a world famous artist who has 100-150 dates in a row and everyday he's in another city. Our USP is the location, the friendship, the quality and the intimacy we offer. Our brand represents history - the recorded live archives of 6,000 hours of music. We are recognised by UNESCO's Memory of the world." (See entry Thierry Amsallem)

The 2014 edition of the MJF had performances by Daptone Super Soul Review, Mavis Staples and Stevie Wonder, among others. It still retained its hallmarks of such good sound, laid-back and friendly atmosphere and presenting superstar acts in what for them is virtually a club-like atmosphere - Stevie Wonder in a 4,000-seat venue. You don't find the carnage of UK festivals here. Besides the paying gigs indoors, the park and lakefront hosted free shows of youth orchestras during the day and Maceo Parker, the funkiest sax player at night. The Rock Cave presented free indie and rock gigs - Toy and Lords of Altamont, while the Jazz Lab had the likes of Ed Sheeran, Lykke Li and London Grammar.

"My advice to young people is to trust yourself, your passion," he said. "Accept what destiny hands you. Sometimes take a step back and listen to yourself."

Mathieu Jaton was left a legacy and there is no doubt that he will build on it. At the European University Commencement Ceremony 2014, he was one of the speakers together with Adolf Ogi, former president of Switzerland. (See entry Dr Dirk Craen). His message was simple. Nothing is impossible in life. You can always beat the odds against you. He himself was promoted to be second-in-command of the MJF at the age of 25. Then in 2013 he became the youngest CEO of a music festival aged 37. He is a shining example to young people today.

When Thierry Met Claude

Thierry Amsallem met Claude Nobs by chance on a train between Lausanne and Montreux in 1987. They clicked instantly and he never left Montreux. Thierry joined him as his partner in Nobs' chalet full of memorabilia like juke boxes, instruments, model trains and art by famous friends like Ronnie Wood, David Bowie and Tony Bennet. It was the 20th anniversary of the Montreux Jazz Festival (MJF) and he was launched into the roller coaster of Nob's life. (See entry Montreux Jazz Festival)

"Claude was a tireless networker and would never take no for an answer," said Thierry. "I was fascinated by the stories of the backgrounds of all the musicians. Who they had played with before they found the right group or sound and became famous. I also learnt how he convinced Aretha Franklin to appear in 1971 with a box of Swiss chocolates. How he forged a lifetime friendship with Miles Davis at the Newport Festival in 1973 by giving him the shirt off his back because the trumpeter liked it. I discovered his nicknames of 'Nobby in the lobby' because he was always awaiting artists in hotels or 'Funky Claude' which was derived from Deep Purple's song Smoke over the water.'"

Thierry was a Parisian who had graduated from the first course in computer science at the university of Paris VI, VII. His credentials were perfect for working alongside Claude. He was technically minded and besides organising recordings, his role was to develop new technology in the music industry.

"We travelled extensively because it was the time of the telex and no internet," said Thierry. "It was important for Claude to meet artists and win their confidence. What they liked about him was that he was a man of his word. If he agreed on something he would stick to it. He reluctantly acceded to Bob Dylan's request in 1994 that the equipment be turned off during his performance. When the singer later requested that he be given the tape of what he considered to be his best concert in 10 years, Claude replied, 'I gave you my word.'"

Nobs was a man of instant connections. He cold-called on the Erteguns in New York at their offices of Atlantic Records because his favourite records from John Coltrane to Ray Charles were produced by them. As it happened, Nesuhi and his younger brother Ahmet had spent time in Switzerland with their Turkish diplomat father. So they welcomed him and played a crucial part in the launch of the Montreux Jazz Festival in 1967.

"I remember when the French illustrator,Tomi Ungerer, was invited to the chalet and Claude was late," said Thierry. "Tomi had so wanted to meet him and was furious. Roger Bornand and I tried to placate him but nothing doing. He went on about wasting his time and about 'how nobody can do this to me.' I rang Claude and he assured me that he was on his way. In the end, Tomi was totally charmed by Claude who also cooked a wonderful meal and the guest stayed for 10 hours. In 2009, he did a poster for the Montreux Jazz Festival to show his appreciation."

David Bowie

They travelled extensively to spread the brand in Brazil, the US and Japan and Claude never lost his child-like wonder or enthusiasm for hearing emerging new groups or old favourites. When they returned, they threw legendary parties at the chalet, Le Picotin, which overlooked Montreux with its spectacular view of lake Geneva. Nobs was a wonderful raconteur

David Bowie at Chalet Le Pictotet ©Claude Nobs private collection

and an amiable host who entertained musicians and friends like Quincy Jones, David Bowie or Phil Collins long into the night. Visitors marveled at the eclectic collection of mementos: A Japanese kimono worn by Freddie Mercury, a print signed by Ronnie Wood of the Rolling Stones and a larger than life bust of Aretha Franklin.

"I was an evangelist of the new and became a catalyst between Apple," said Thierry, "which wanted to enter the music world and Warner who had the musicians. I also was a go-between the musicians and Apple which had the technology to download music. Some musicians were suspicious because they were afraid people could steal their music. Quincy Jones was one of the few who understood."

In 1991, Apple introduced the QuickTime player which was a breakthrough for multimedia and it was followed three years later by a music track playback that transcended existing computer audio quality. QuickTime eventually grew into Apple's default video playback programme which still exists today. iPod which was next in 2001 snowballed into the premier digital music gadget and 2003, iTunes store.

"My achievement is the complete digitalisation of the archives," said Thierry. "When Patrick Aebischer, president of EPFL, came to see us in the chalet, he was introduced to the archives of 5,000 hours of live recordings after 40 years. He was surprised that only one original copy existed. I was keen to have the recordings digitalized and Claude persuaded him to explore the idea of creating a Montreux Jazz Lab at EPFL. The idea is being implemented and will open in 2015. In the ultra longterm, it would be great to have a platform for memories of the festival."

During his time with MJF, he had the opportunity of hearing many great musicians. The ones he liked were those who sang from the gut for example, Marvin Gaye. David Bowie is a real artist but not from this world and Prince is one of the sexiest performers.

"If I am asked what advice I would give to a young person," he said, "my reply would be: think about yourself. Try to find something you love to do and do it! You'll find more energy that way. Life is too short."

Thierry has established the Claude Nobs Foundation with the goal of preserving and making accessible to the greatest number of people the compendium of live recordings. The performers at the festival have once been described by Nobs like a rainbow of different music, a combination of the different components found in the Swiss muesli. The year before Claude died, he was asked about the future of the MJF. "I have a team of people who are all set to take over the festival," he replied. "I think Montreux has established itself well enough that it can continue without me."

"The highlight of my life with Claude and my involvement with the MJF is the recognition given to us by UNESCO," he said. "In June 2013, the archives were inscribed in the Memory of the World Programme because of their historical value as an exceptional witness of the 20th century music."

Collector Extraordinaire

Roger Bornand who lives in Montreux established his graphic studio in the same year as Claude Nobs founded the Montreux Jazz Festival. In fact, his first client was the Festival and he designed their first poster.

"I'd returned from a trip of 30,000 miles in the USA in 1967," he said, "San Francisco and its hippie culture had impressed me a lot. The poster for the Festival benefitted and had a psychedelic style. I ended up doing the job for nothing as Nobs didn't have any funds."

Roger who studied graphic design and attended an executives course in Lausanne, expanded his business over the years and today, it is a successful advertising, digital and PR agency with a turnover of CHF 5 million. Among the clients he had were Caterpillar, Migros, Alinghi, Inter Ikea and Médecins Sans Frontières. Besides a talent for copywriting and design - once an advert in a newspaper for new homes sold out immediately, he was also a passionate collector. But his tastes vary widely from autographs, to slot machines and funfair art. In his autographed documents, he is particularly proud of the handwritten inaugural speech which Pope Pius VIII gave in 1819 at St John de Lateran Cathedral in Rome. Some of 50 slot machines which cover 1897 to the 1950s are now in the Swiss Museum of Games, La Tour de Peilz. Among funfair objects are a shooting gallery and a barrel organ. There is another collection which he treasures above all else. It's a gift which Claude Nobs gave him shortly before his death - books on advertising in the 1950s and 1960s.

"When I'm asked what advice to give young people," he said, "it's an easy answer. Open your mind through traveling. See what happens in other places. When I went to America in 1967, it was a determinant. I realised that everything was possible. Here in Switzerland things are too restricted through bureaucracy."

Roger is proud of living in Montreux. On Facebook, he has posted over 1,400 old photos of the city from 1860. He also likes to tell you that the Montreux Riviera is good for the health and wellbeing. To substantiate his case, he cites the fact that in 1829, 29 doctors resided there to take care of the visitors who had come for a cure.

Gilbert & George

Anne Rapin-Zurcher is the fifth generation to run the Confiserie Zurcher. Her descendant, Arnold Zurcher, was born in Emmental and trained to become a confectioner. He established the tearoom in 1879 in the avenue du Casino.

"My great, great grandfather had heard that Montreux was being developed," said Anne Rapin, "and when he arrived he fell in love with the resort. Eventually, the family bought the property where we are today. But it was much larger and we even had a restaurant at the other end."

Ann has a strong sense of family and has dedicated her life to running the confiserie. There was no family pressure to follow in their footsteps. She trained as a baker and then studied at the Geneva Hotel Management School. When she graduated she worked for the Accor Hotels group for five years. She changed direction and went into sport events management. But eventually returned to the family business.

"As a child of four or five, I would stand on a box so that I could reach the table and help my mother, Antoinette and grandfather, Edouard in the confiserie," she said. "I've happy memories with my grandfather. Every Saturday, he would fetch me and we would go to the basement to make icing sugar together. I would watch him pour sugar into the top of the machine and then wait for the fine powder to emerge at the bottom. I liked the warm smell of the icing which appeared like a cloud.

"I'm pleased that we still make classical cakes such as the marguerite flower," she added. "It's made with the old machine from my great grandfather's time. And what's funny is that one of my girlfriends still expects me to bring them marguerites on their birthdays 30 years later as I did when I was a little girl."

Easter is always an exciting time for her because one of the retired artisans returns to create the rabbits. She likes to watch him work because he strives to customize

From left Antoinette Zurcher, Anne Rapin-Zurcher

them. No eyes are the same nor the mouths or ears. For her a beautiful thing about the job is to see the happy expressions on the faces of the customers when they look at a row of rabbits. Wow!

Rothko

Anne is also moved by paintings. Some 10 years ago, she saw the Rothko exhibition at the Tate Modern in London and was overcome by a very strong emotion. It was like listening to music. There was no pretension involved. She is a fan of the artists Gilbert and George and one day posed herself and her mother in a similar tableau.

When Anne joined in 2005, one of the first tasks was to work with the master confectioner Max Müller and learn about the secret recipes. She wanted to continue the traditional range of chocolates and patisserie. With the confiserie it includes the specialties which speak of the region like little chocolate fish with nougat, the stones, meringues, the corks of Vaud, among other chocoholics treats. There is a delicious choice from the rum baba with a little pipette of rum, fruit tarts with seasonal fruit to a new range of contemporary patisserie by Philippe Blondiaux.

"My grandfather decided to renovate the tearoom in 1969," she said, " a work which took three years. Later, when I joined my mother in running it, I was full of ideas to change things. It was hard work because we had 360 seats as the tearoom included a restaurant at the back which had terrace with a magnificent view of the lake and mountains. But later, I realised that in spite of my new ideas, I also had the role of a guardian of 135 years of family history. Our first radical change came after my grandmother, Dora's death when we decided to close the restaurant and convert it into two apartments. The next change came when I took over the family enterprise because I wanted my own place."

Anne first had reservations about the new development as she was concerned about the reaction of the customers. Many of them were habitués who came every day to have coffee or lunch and even had their respective tables. Some had been customers for over 30 years. However, she was reassured when one longstanding customer revealed that in spite of the changes, Anne had kept the soul and atmosphere of the place. There are now four distinct interiors in the tearoom.

"My mother and I visited all sorts of tearooms to get ideas and be inspired," she said. "First of all we wanted to create an atmosphere of chaleureux or cosiness and to give a warm welcome to all types of people. So customers have a choice of seating. If they want an experience of the sidewalk cafes in Paris, they sit near the window. If they want old fashioned comfortable upholstered seating, its in the second area. In the third, we have original furniture from the past so that newcomers can get a feeling of what it was like and some older people would feel comfortable. The last area is furnished with contemporary armchairs and sofas and coffee tables and has a fireplace."

Her first export order went to Australia. But it began in an odd way. An Australian bought two boxes of chocolates to take back to Sydney. One was for him and the other for a friend. A couple of weeks later, she received a telephone call from him.

"He was upset," she said. "because he had put the two boxes of chocolates on the kitchen table and his dog had eaten the one for his friend. He wanted to order one more box. I said I would check about the transport costs and ring him back. Indeed, I found that the postage was CHF 70 compared to the chocolates which was only CHF 26. But he was determined to go through with it. Then one of my staff told me that an Australian woman was flying back to Australia and she might agree to take a box back in her luggage. I spoke to the woman and she was delighted to help. When she saw the address which was near her home, she agreed to deliver it personally. That's how I fulfilled my first export order."

Her mother, Anoinette is a charming woman and although she is retired from the business comes for lunch each day. "I feel it's important for Anne to have a break during the busy day. We both take time over the lunch."

She has anecdotes about customers. One was about the tall elegant Mrs Nabokov, the author's wife who lived with her husband in a suite of rooms at the Fairmont Le Montreux Palace hotel. "She would ring me up once a week about her order," said Antoinette. Everybody would know what the Nabokov's selection of bread and patisserie was in Zurcher because she shouted the order down the phone. She was deaf. Another regular was an English woman Mrs Acciaioli who always rang to check on the plat du jour in advance. If there was something she didn't like we would know and remove it when she was served later."

In the 1950s and 1960s, Montreux was a great place for the young. They would be sleeping the park, hanging their washing on the branches of the trees and brushing their teeth as they walked around. The Montreux Jazz festival began in 1968. David Bowie, Chris Rea, Queen, Duran Duran all had their records engineered and produced at Mountain studios by the owner, David Richards.

"I remember when David Bowie had his coffee there. Once a teenager who was too shy to ask for his autograph walked past his table three times and before he disappeared."

Anne Rapin is a shining example of Swiss womanhood who are the backbone of the hospitality industry in Switzerland. Managing cafes or restaurants were not considered to be suitable for men. So she followed her mother into the family enterprise and in 2009 became the principal owner after her mother's retirement. She has no children but 26 staff, one of whom came back in his retirement to make artistic Easter bunnies. Her greatest compliment is when a customer tells her that the high quality of the products are still maintained over 30 years. She is proud of the achievements of the family and is certain that her grandfather would approve of Zurcher today."

The Stones Came to Dinner

François Michel who is the Vice President and Marketing Director of Lake Geneva Region was born in Montreux but grew up in Vevey. Like all the youth in the 1970s, he was a fan of the Montreux Jazz Festival. It was a great time. François was fortunate as he became part of the inner circle of the MJF. The founder, Claude Nobs, took him under his wing and became his mentor.

"One evening, there was a big party at Claude Nob's chalet," he said, "when the Rolling Stones came to dinner. It was an exciting moment for me but you had to act 'natural.' I was also fortunate to meet other major groups, among them ELP, YES, David Bowie – they were all coming to Montreux to record albums at the then famous Mountain Recording Studio which was housed in the Montreux Casino."

François comes from an old Vevey family and his father worked for the electricity company in Montreux. He went to high school and later studied at the commercial school in Lausanne.

"I was supposed to become an accountant," he said, "but I was attracted to music and tourism. Michel Ferla who together with Claude Nobbs worked at the Montreux Tourism office, gave me my first job as a ski instructor for American groups. We used Montreux as a base and each day went to different ski resorts such as Zermatt. In 1977, I was given the responsibility to handle all ticket sales for the MJF. At that time, everything was done manually!"

From 1977-1980, he worked as book-keeper for Montreux Sounds. It was founded by Claude Nobs and provided services for the three recording labels of Warner Communications in Europe. In 1980, he was appointed Sales Manager of Montreux Tourism where he remained until 1995.

"I had always wanted to travel to the US," he said, "and when Michel Ferla was appointed director of the Montreux Tourism, I was given that opportunity. My brief was to promote meetings, incentives, conferences and events (MICE). Michel Ferla was also my mentor. He inspired me with confidence. Once you won his trust, he would never let you down. Of course, there were moments when we had differences of opinion but even then he gave me the opportunity of proving myself. My other mentor, Claude Nobbs was a different kettle of fish. He was a person to whom you couldn't say no as he was very persuasive. I learnt to listen to people and come up with solutions rather than problems."

In 1995, François landed the plum position of Vice President and Marketing director of Office du Tourisme du Canton du Vaud. It provided him with a global reach for not only was he promoting Vaud Canton as destination for MICE but also leisure tourism. During almost two decades in the position, he has opened up new markets worldwide as well as introduced the attractions of Vaud. Apropos the Montreux Riviera, he highlights the fact that there are many activities on your doorstep - hiking in the Lavaux vineyards, skiing in the Alps and swimming in the lake. He also reveals special places known to locals like the fantastic trail along the Gorge du Cloudron (above Montreux) where you end up in the middle of the forest near a river; the breathtaking view from the auberge du Souchoux (above Veytraux); the beach at La Crottaz on chemin de la paix below Corseaux; and the Saturday market in Place du Marché, Vevey where you can sit on a terrace with a glass of Chasselas and enjoy the ambiance.

"My advice for anyone who wants to start a career in tourism," he said, "is to listen to people before you try to give advice. And when you do, be honest. The key is that you have to earn a person's confidence if you want them to buy something you're selling."

Pleasing Others

Michael Smithuis who is the General manager of the Fairmont Le Montreux Palace is a hotelier par excellence. "What is important to me is job satisfaction. This derives from the guests through their positive feedback and from staff when I see smiles on their faces."

Today 5-star hotels proliferate around the world and almost all offer similar luxurious services which are an accoutrement of their status. But few have a long reach of the Fairmont Le Montreux Palace where you experience the grandness of the Belle Epoque style and with a little imagination mingle with the European aristocrats, Russian princes and maharajahs or rub shoulders with Richard Strauss, Vladimir Nabokov or Freddie Mercury, some of the numerous celebrated guests. Where else can you find a choice of 236 rooms and suites including Nabokov's suite in the Cygne wing where he stayed with his wife Vera. And what of the 15 meeting and banquet rooms which can cater for 1,200 people including the Salles des Fêtes where 500 diplomats were present at the signing of the Montreux Convention which gave Turkey control over the Bosporus and the Dardanelles straits in 1936.

Michael Smithuis was born in Hengelo, Holland, a place which stimulates travel for it is on the Amsterdam to Berlin train route and the Amsterdam to Moscow motorway. The town is home to notable people like Henk Kamp who is a government minister, the artist Theo Wolvecamp and now a renowned hotelier.

"After school I decided to train as a hotelier in Germany," said Michael Smithuis. "The first step was at the Steigenberger hotel school in Bad Reichenhall. After a year, I needed practical experience and went to London where I worked at the Mayfair InterContinental hotel. I started at the bottom as a waiter, then head night waiter and in room service. It was a hotel that I was to return again and again for work experience."

He continued his education in hospitality and hotel management by attending the International Hotel and Tourism Training Institute (IHTTI) in Neuchatel. He graduated in 1991 and returned to the Mayfair where he occupied different positions in F & B and later moved to the Front Office department as Night manager and Assistant Manager.

Sultan Qaboos

"After various positions in London, I was ready to broaden my horizon with travel," he said, "and discover the world of global hospitality in different countries, cultures and religions. I was given the opportunity within InterContinental in Oman where I was appointed as Assistant Front Office Manager in the Al Bustan Palace hotel. The hotel with its 250 rooms and suites is set on a private beach with lush gardens and near the capital Muscat. The country is ruled by Sultan Qaboos and the Omanis consist of many different ethnic groups."

Michael stayed for two years in Oman before he was promoted to Front Office Manager at the Stuttgart InterContinental hotel in Germany. It provided him with the basic tools of operating a hotel. Again after two years, he switched his career radically and left InterContinental for the Mandarin Oriental Group in Jakarta. It was an Asian luxury brand which was based on service excellence and the unique oriental feel and ambience. Jakarta was a former Dutch colony and is nicknamed the big Durian, the thorny foul- smelling fruit.

"I was excited by my new appointment as Executive Assistant Manager," he said. "I was now at the helm of a 423 roomed Leading Hotel in the world, working with the General Manager. It had different standards and ways of doing things. The mission was to delight and satisfy our guests every day. Also, I had to invest time with the staff, many of whom had little education and lived in poor conditions. One of the things I learnt was to treat people of different cultures and religions with respect."

Michael was again on his two-year cycle of change and in 1998, he switched to the Raffles Hotels and Resorts chain. This time it was not for a position in the east but in the west. He was appointed Resident Manager of the Raffles Hotel Vier Jahreszeiten Hotel, Hamburg.

"I took part in the rebranding of the famous hotel," he said. "I stayed just over three years before joining the Corporate Head Office in Singapore as Corporate Director. My assignment was to work with the Chairman and President of Raffles Hotels and Resorts on the acquisition of Swissôtel Hotels and Resorts, comprising 23 operational hotels worldwide, across six continents and 17 countries."

Michael's next big challenge was to return to his homeland where he managed the Swissôtel Amsterdam. He was also appointed the Regional director of Operations for Europe, Middle East and the Mediterranean. When Fairmont merged with Raffles Hotels and Resorts, he was given the plum position of General Manager of the Grand old Lady, the Fairmont Le Montreux Palace. Now he could put his wide experience and talent as a hotelier to good use. Again he was asked to do a re-branding of the Hotel and CHF 110 million has been spent on renovation of the guest rooms and public areas.

"After some 15 years of travelling between continents and cities," said Michael, "I finally settled in Montreux where I have been for over a decade. I'm proud of the achievements since then and I'm always kept busy through company and personal goals. Even when I jog - I cover 36 km a week, I give myself two issues to think about and solve. What is important to me is job satisfaction. This derives from the guests through their positive feedback and from staff when I see smiles on their faces."

Since Michael Smithuis arrived at the hotel it has won over 30 awards including the Best of the Best Conde Nast Traveller Gold List 2007 and the European Hotel Award for the Best hotel in Switzerland in 2013. Awards are one thing but he never rests on his laurels and is always finding ways to improve. For someone who has worked his way from being a waiter to the GM of a great hotel, his advice to students is simple: "Treat people with respect and look for longterm success and not short term."

Bollywood

Naseem Merali has the poise and looks of a Bollywood movie star. Indeed her life could be turned into a scenario. Her great grandfather's dhows traded along the east coast of Africa with cargoes of spices, cotton, coffee and tea. The family settled in Kenya and the home port for the dhows was Mombasa.

"I grew up in a large 'colonial-type' house in the capital, Nairobi," she said. " It was surrounded by a big garden. Fruit dropped from the trees - mangoes, guavas, passion fruit, pawpaws. It was like Karen Blixen's "Out of Africa". I had four brothers and I was the only girl. My father treated me like the fifth son. We spent a lot of time in the library where he educated me. I read Shakespeare, Charles Dickens and Oscar Wilde. He pushed me hard and I became self-sufficient and a fighter. But I was also feminine."'

She first attended Lord Delamere's school and then was sent to boarding school - Queensway College in England. When Kenya achieved independence, the Merali family who had British/Kenyan passports left to live in the UK. Later, she studied hospitality management and tourism in the UK. After her diploma, she came to Montreux to learn French.

"When I ended my French course, I was told that a job was being advertised at the Montreux Tourist and Convention Bureau," said Naseem. "At the time, it was difficult for a foreigner to get a work permit. Nevertheless, I got all dolled up and went to see Raymond Jaussi, the head of Montreux Tourism. He was impressed with the way I looked and even more so when he heard my posh English accent and my profile just fitted the job which was being offered. I was hired on the spot as the office had one permit for the Montreux Tourist and Convention Bureau."

Although, the job was her first break, she was hampered by the Mr Jaussi's idea that women were only good in operations and not in sales. Eventually, she had an opportunity when one of the male

Naseem Merali

colleagues became sick and could not attend a Convention and Tourism Fair(ITME) in Atlanta, Georgia.

"I was asked to go in his place," she said. "I remember the venue clearly – it was in an Exhibition Centre near the Peachtree Plaza. On the first evening at 16.45 I was setting up the stand when five guys appeared. They were from the American Oil Chemists Society, Champagne, Illinois. They were interested in organising a soap and detergent conference in Switzerland as the counterpart and host company was based in Zurich. My heart was thumping when I learnt that they had 800 delegates. I told them I'd check and do a presentation the next day. That night I couldn't sleep. All the dates for the conference and accommodation were available. It's amazing as I was the right person, at the right place at the right time. And even more incredible as I still have those clients today. Their 8th conference took place this October! At the Tourist Office, I was nicknamed "Chausses de Congrès!"

In 1998, Naseem was offered a position at the Fairmont Le Montreux Palace hotel as Sales operations and Events manager. She has been there ever since.

"In 2012, I was asked to prepare an event for the 'Montreux Top Events' with the stipulation that I also had to be present," she said. "Halfway through the proceedings, I heard my name mentioned and realised that I had won the 'Montreux Top Events' Award"'.

1

If Naseem had any mentors, it's her father and Benazir Bhutto. She met Prime Minister of Pakistan at a time when both their mothers were dying and bonded. A woman who has charm at her fingertips, she won trust from her clients through her caring, outgoing manners and her efficiency.

"My advice to young women is to be humble and also assertive in business," she said. "But never neglect your looks."

Montreux Grand Prix

Ezio Vialmin who lives in Montreux is part of the new generation in hospitality. He runs the same restaurant as his parents but in a totally different style. He is hands-on and delegates to his team. He relies on them whereas his parents relied only on each other and were in two places at once. It was only by chance that he took over the restaurant some 15 years ago. He was a highflyer at Mövenpick and was scheduled to go to Cairo for a top position when he changed his mind.

"My parents told me that they were going to retire and sell the business," he said. "It was final and there was no pressure on me at any time to take over the restaurant. I stopped in my tracks and thought this was crazy. I'd grown up in Montreux, I'd loved the resort, I'd gained good experience at places like the Gstaad Palace and Gavroche in London, worked for chains like Hilton, Accor and Mövenpick. Why not stay and take over the restaurant from them."

It was a good decision because he was able to express his managerial and leadership skills as well as the entrepreneurial side of his personality. As a result, he established a hotel next to the restaurant and an ice cream shop around the corner. With a friend he bought the oldest restaurant in Vevey, the Avenir. It specialises in fondues and is popular with the locals. A student can be seated near an executive from Nestlé.

"You're not alone in life, everyone needs someone to evolve," he said. "My chef is an expert with cooking; Massimo is my sommelier who has a passion for wine; the pizzaoilo makes the bread, fresh pasta and pizzas; Indira is the restaurant manager but at the end everyone is important. I sit down with them and we all decide the budget together. My policy in the Rouvinaz is to cater for all pockets so you can have a pizza for CHF 17 or a menu at CHF 70."

"You need to take a chance when you start a business," he added. "Above all you need to believe in yourself and want to succeed. But part of the deal is luck. But it's not easy every day because I never finish my work. I always want to do something better. My philosophy is Vivre et laisser vivre or live and let live. I find that nowadays it's increasingly difficult carry out because regulations are blocking creativity."

Ezio has another passion besides hospitality. It's classic and racing cars and he is the president of the Montreux Grand Prix. The event started as a race in 1934 which was won by the Count Felice Trossi in a Alfa Romeo. On the occasion, part of the excitement was the duel between the French pilot Philippe Etancelin in a Maserati and the Alfa Romeo team directed by Enzo Ferrari. However, because of the dangers to the audience in car racing in recent years, the Grand Prix has been transformed into an exhibition and parade of the classic cars.

"I took over as the president in 2002 as I like classic cars from the 1950s and 1960s," said Ezio. "Now we do events every two years and in 2014, we'll celebrate the 80th anniversary. When I was younger I was great fan of Niki Lauder, Ayrton Senna, Clay Reggazoni and Michael Schumacher. Clay Reggazoni who became a friend and a godfather of the Montreux Grand Prix, ate regularly at the Rouvenaz."

Ezio's other interest is the history of Montreux. He enthuses over the three men who transformed Montreux from a series of small villages into a famous resort. There was Eugene Jost the architect, Ami Chessex the businessman and hotelier who owned the hotel des Alpes, Territet and his brother-in-law, Alexandre Emery another hotelier who was the initiator of the Montreux Palace. They built the Caux Palace which was the largest hotel in Europe. He is proud of the origin of the name Rouvenaz which either came from the family who lived in the area or the slope of the land. It was only in 1961 that Montreux became the administrative head of the surrounding villages.

"And our job in Montreux hospitality," he said as a parting remark, "is to assure the future for the next generation."

Hospitality Generates Success

Back in 2000 Dr Andreas Künzli ran a hospitality school with one building, one campus and 400 students. Then 14 years later the school had expanded beyond recognition to 29 buildings, seven campuses and 5,500 students. The reason? Florent Rondez had joined him as his right hand in the management team of what is now the Swiss Education group (SEG).

Florent was born in La Chaux de Fonds and came from a family who were involved in the restaurant industry. One of his earliest memories is waiting on the tables at his uncle's restaurant. When he grew older, he had more experience in all aspects of running a restaurant and found that he was passionate about cooking.

"In fact, I enjoyed the hospitality from A to Z," said Florent Rondez who is the CEO of SEG. "I relish discovering new features in the hospitality industry. When I stayed at the Peninsula Beverly Hills, I found a pillow embroidered with my initials instead of the usual bottle of champagne. It was most memorable and I now have three pillows as souvenirs. On a trip to Korea, I discovered another incredible innovation, during my stay at the W hotel in Walkerhill, Seoul. When I arrived, I checked in at reception. Later, it was turned into a bar and then in the evening into a night club."

Florent was impatient to study at the Lausanne Hospitality School and applied at the age of 14. There was a long waiting list and even so it took two years longer before he could enroll as a student.

"When I graduated in 1993, it was difficult to find a job in Switzerland," he said, "I instead landed up at the fantastic Mandarin Oriental Group in Macao. I started as a management trainee but after a few months I was promoted to manager. I was at the job for 18 months and then moved to Hong Kong where I stayed for six years. I tended to change jobs every 18-24 months and my last position was at Maxims where I was F & B director of the European division of the group. In 2000, I had reached the point in my life when I wanted to change my life radically. My aim was to open a shop. When nothing worked out, I instead applied for the position of Operations manager at the Swiss Hospitality and Management School (SHMS) which was established in 1992 and in the former Caux Palace hotel."

He became the right hand of Dr Andreas Künzli and played a notable role in the evolution of SHMS into SEG. Today, it consists of five schools in both the French and German speaking areas of Switzerland. Each school is based in a former hotel which has been modernised to provide one of the best facilities for hotel management and culinary studies in Switzerland. SEG has grown into a world leading hospitality network and includes Cesar Ritz colleges, Culinary Arts Academy, Hotel Institute Montreux, International Hotel and Tourism Training Institute (IHTTI) and the Swiss Hotel Management School (SHMS).

"One of the many advantages of SEG is that we work closely with the industry and other prestigious brands," he said, "and in fact companies are given the opportunity to participate in our educational programme. It's important for the students to be close to reality and for the industry to teach them what they require. For example, among the lecturers we've had are executives from the Ritz Paris Hotel, Edmond de Rothschild private bank and Accor Group.

Once a year, before graduation SEG organises one of the largest job fairs in Switzerland with over 60 companies such as Hyatt, Kempinsky, Raffles, Hilton, Four Seasons, Swiss Air and many more. Afterwards, graduates are welcomed into the alumni network with over 20,000 members worldwide. These networks help graduates to stay in touch and expand their networking opportunities.

"The key element to success is to establish a powerful team with the same goal," he said, "which can be achieved through strong leadership. I spend about two months out of the year travelling worldwide to attend some 25-30 alumni parties and to liaise with recruiters of students, Swiss representatives abroad and hoteliers."

Florent Rondez's world of hospitality consists of food and music. He is also passionate about cooking. But above all, he believes that if you study hospitality, you are fit to run any business. It will open many doors in the global village.

Museums and Art Galleries

Chillon Castle

Avenue de Chillon 21
1820 Veytaux
Tel 021 966 8910
info@chillon.ch
www.chillon.ch

Chillon Castle is the most famous landmark in the Montreux Riviera and the most visited historic monument in Switzerland. What accounts for the Chillon's international popularity is that it's the most beautiful preserved medieval castle in a stunning setting of lake Geneva and the Alps.

The castle is fascinating because visitors gain an insight into what it was like to live there in the 13th century. The most imposing feature is the tall watch tower or keep which is 31 metres high. It was the last refuge in case the castle was besieged and had secret passage to escape outside.

Once visitors enter the castle, they will find four courtyards on the defensive side which runs along the road. Each courtyard is higher than the next. The lowest is where the servants and stables were housed and the second was for the castellan or governor. But the most important courtyard was at the third level where the Duke of Savoy and his family lived. The focus is the window which was in the form of a cross and was painted in blue while the rest of the castle was in white. The fourth courtyard was used by the militia to defend the castle and has a view the street towards the bridge.

Inside the castle, the most popular room is the dungeon where François Bonivard was imprisoned for four years and where Lord Byron carved his name on a pillar. Each of the living quarters of the castellan and the Savoy family had a bedroom and two reception rooms. The Duke's bedroom is of particular interest as it has not been restored and the original paintings can be seen on the walls. There is St George who was the protector of the family and the ceiling was decorated with precious metals like silver and gold. Here you also can see the window of the cross.

The interior of the castle is a splendid affair with halls, parts of original furniture and ceilings, stoves and twin seated wooden toilets with deep drops into the lake. The two periods of occupation, the Savoy and the Bernese can be seen immediately through the different room decorations. The simple patterns belonged to the Savoyards while the complicated designs of flowers to the Bernese.

Chillon castle was built in the 12th century on a rocky outcrop in lake Geneva and served as fortress and its strategic position enabled the Dukes of Savoy to control traffic between the north and south of Europe. There were three major periods in the history of the castle. The Savoy was the first from the 12th century until 1536 and the oldest document in 1150 stated that they controlled the route along the shores of lake Geneva. In 1214, Thomas I of Savoy founded the town of Villeneuve where a tollbooth, warehouses for storage of goods and port facilities were sited. Their vast territory covered Vaud, the

1

Chateau Chillon

Dungeon Chateau Chillon

lower Valais, the southern shore of lake Geneva to Evian and Thonon and included what is now the Savoie and Haut-Savoie departments of France. It consisted of several bailliages and the governor of the castle took on the duties of the bailiff of Chablais. To maintain a close relationship with their subjects, the Savoy family tended to travel around their extensive territory. As befitted the Duke, he was accompanied by his court, an entourage and took along furniture and equipment needed to furnish the residences where he stayed. They remained empty during his absences. There is a lasting memorial in Champéry, Valais, as the inhabitants fashioned the belfry of St Theodule in the shape of the Duke of Savoy's crown as a token of affection and esteem.

When the Bernese army of 6,000 soldiers commanded by Hans-Franz Naegeli conquered Vaud in 1536, Chillon fell into their hands. The castle retained its role as fortress and arsenal and prison for over 260 years. It became the administrative centre for the bailliage of Vevey and permanent residence for the bailiff. Then 1733, the bailiffs left as it no longer served its purpose for military operations and the castle was used for storage purposes.

The third period, the Vaudois, began in 1798 when the Bernese left at the time of the Vaudois revolution. The castle became the property of the canton of Vaud when it was founded in 1803. At first, the castle was again used as a storage for gunpowder, munitions and weapons and also as a prison. In 1816, Lord Byron brought the castle to prominence through his poem, The Prisoner of Chillon. His account recalls the sufferings of François Bonivard (1493-1570), prior of Saint-Victor, Geneva and politician. He was imprisoned there from 1530-1536 by Charles III, Duke of Savoy, because of his opposition and liberated by the Bernese. He had spent four years in chains in the dungeon and became a symbol of liberty. The prison in Chillon became a place of pilgrimage. In time, the canton of Vaud relented over their indifference and replaced the guards with guides as the tourists kept coming in increasing numbers.

The reason for its popularity was simple because a grisly tale had been concocted by prison guards, the guides and Lord Byron. Bonivard's father and brother had been burnt at the stake, two brothers had died in the battlefield while two other brothers had died pining away. But despite the fable about Bonivard, there was a basis for terror because Chillon had a reputation for burning witches, hangings and torturing prisoners both during the Savoy and Bernese periods. And even today, ropes are hung from beams to emulate gallows to continue the grisly reputation.

"Most people are aware that the House of Savoy controlled the passes in the Alps between France and Italy," said Jean Pierre Pastori, director of Chillon Castle, "but what they don't know is that the cultivation of the arts was a prerogative too of the family. Music was the foremost of the arts at their court. Indeed in 1433, when Louis the son of first Duke of Savoy, Amadeus VIII, married Anne, a Lusignan princess, Guillaume Dufay who was the eminent musician of the day, composed music for the wedding. Both Louis and his wife Anne played the harp and part of her trousseau was manuscript that contained a wide selection of works from the late 14th to the early 15th centuries. Courtly songs, love songs and spring songs must have soothed the nostalgia of the Duchess."

Alongside music, painting was another form of art used by the Savoyards and the walls and panels of their castle were decorated as well as the illumination of manuscripts. A unique masterpiece, the heart-shaped song book which was copied in Savoy in about 1470 contains fashionable compositions by Dufay and others and is now held by the Bibliothèque Nationale in Paris.

Jean Pierre Pastori was born in Lausanne and studied political science at the University of Lausanne before beginning a career in journalism. He wrote his first article for the Geneva Tribune at the age of 17. He worked for radio and television Suisse Romande (RSR) from 1972 -1995 before he was appointed administrator of the orchestra Sinfonietta de Lausanne where he stayed until 1999. His next position was as director and editor for the local television of Lausanne (TVRL) until 2007. Then he had a sea change in his career and joined Chillon Castle. He went from the fourth estate to the patrician with his appointment as director. But although he could live as a castellan in the castle, he waived the privilege and instead preferred to commute to his home in Lausanne.

"I was one of the 70 candidates for the job and I was chosen," he said with insouciance, "but then it was always my dream to be in a castle. I am sure that my cultural background with books on dance and music and my lifelong interest in ballet helped."

He is the author of 20 publications and books which include ballet and biographies on Charles Dutoit and Serge Lifar. He came to dance through his mentor at RSR, Antoine Livio, who introduced him to the subject and then left for Paris. His current literary project is on the Swiss couturier, Robert Piguet who trained Dior and Givenchy and died in 1953. He is also studying the lesser known member of the Surrealists, René Crevel. Ultimately, Pastori's cultural interests resulted in him being awarded a Chevalier des arts et des lettres in 1999.

"Dance was an untapped niche," said Pastori, "and I got into it and acquired the taste. Now I have an opportunity again as I can fill the courtyards of Chillon with dance and music." Then added tongue-in-cheek, "It's like a recreation of the cultural court of the House of Savoy."

Pastori has his offices in the first courtyard of the servants and horses. His office has an ancient bay window seat which looks straight down into the lake. He exudes good humour and bonhomie and is in his element. For he, like the House of Savoy has a grand area for entertainment and culture. There is an opportunity for him to play the role of castellane in a castle which has inspired artists and writers from Delacroix to Courbet, from Jean-Jacques

Rousseau to Byron and Victor Hugo who called it a "block of towers sitting on a block of rocks." He is also proud of the Visitor's book which includes not only a descendant of the Dukes of Savoy - Princess Maria Gabriella of Savoy and of Lord Byron - the Honourable Caroline Anne Victoria Byron but also Queen Elizabeth II and the Duke of Edinburgh, Salvador Dali and the pop star, Rod Stewart.

When a visitor looks down at the lake from the bay window seat, it is an opportunity for Pastori to discuss the experiment of immersion of bottles of Clos de Chillon wine at 23 metres below the castle. It will investigate how a wine reacts to constant temperature in the dark humid environment and with a low oxygen level. It is a joint project with Badoux wine in Aigle. At last Chillon Castle has found a latter-day counterpart to the original owners.

Museum of Old Montreux

Rue de la Gare 40
Tel 021 9631353
museemontreux@bluewin.ch
www.museemontreux.ch

The museum is found in the old town among the zigzagging streets and steep terraces. It has exhibitions on four themes: history, landscape, tourism and hospitality. Among the variety of objects are a collection of over 2,000 thimbles.

Laurent Marthaler Gallery

Fairmont Le Montreux Palace Avenue
Claude Nobbs Montreux
Tel 021 963 1122
info@laurentmarthaler.com
www.laurentmarthaler.com

Laurent Marthaler who lives in Montreux is a gallerist to watch on the international art scene. He is a latter-day Ambroise Vollard who can do the same for Swiss artists as the French art dealer did for Cezanne and other French painters.

"I am prepared to defend the work of my artists in a similar way as Vollard," he said. "He rescued Cezanne from obscurity in 1895 when he had the courage to mount a ground-breaking exhibition of the unknown artist. I'm not promoting them or advertising their work but giving a good reason why they have outstanding talent. Gilles Rotzetter is one of them."

If there is anyone who is qualified to understand artistic competence then it's Laurent. He has a MA in Art History from Geneva university and was a senior in the exchange programme of the university of Florence. His thesis was the Gothic medieval theme of epiphany. Besides his academic background, he has had a good all round commercial experience - at an auction house, with a private collector in Argentina, as an art appraiser, a curator and principally with an international art gallery group, Fine Art Invest. There he was exposed to modern and contemporary art, management practices including PR and logistics and organised exhibitions in Europe and the Middle East."

"My picture moment came at the age of 11 at the Kunsthistorisches museum in Vienna," he said. "I stood before *The Miracles of St Francis Xavier by Rubens* and was gobsmacked by its monumentality - its height was 18 feet and width 13 feet. I didn't understand that human beings could do that."
Peter Paul Rubens was a Flemish painter who delighted in undertakings of the vastest size. He believed that the large size of the picture gave painters more courage to represent their ideas with utmost freedom and semblance of reality. He created *The Miracles of St Francis Xavier* in 1617-1618.

"With the development of digital art and galleries on the net, there is a feeling that museums are passé," he said. "But I totally agree with Winckelmann that museums are to art what temples are to religion. I love to go to the Guggenheim and see masterpieces. With contemporary art, I like to be seduced and surprised and with classical art, I transcend. Whenever, I visit the Louvre my starting point is always the sculpture, Canova's Psyche revived by Cupid's kiss."

The Laurent Marthaler Gallery which is found at the Fairmont Le Montreux Palace specialises in contemporary art. It has five to six solo exhibitions a year as well as a group exhibition each summer. Part of the service it offers is to select acquisitions for companies as well as private collectors. Some of the companies Laurent has worked with include Credit Suisse, AXA Assurance and Julius Baer. His artists had already collaborated with them.

"The hardest part for any private collector is to buy the first artwork," he said. "I call it spilling your blood. It often starts when a person buys for decoration or to fill a space on the wall. But the next stage is to sharpen your mind which with art is analogous to a diamond. It starts off rough but in time becomes polished. Once you've made the decision on an artwork, get to know the artist and his world. Never be afraid to buy."

One of Laurent's favourite dealers is Lord Duveen who persuaded Paul Mellon to gift the National Gallery in Washington DC to the American nation in lieu of paying outstanding taxes. Once Mellon had made his gift, Duveen was on hand to advise him on what Old Masters he should purchase to fill the gallery.

"The reason for dealing in contemporary art is that it has always has always been a reflection of the world," he said. "Through the artist's idea you can see things with a critical eye and enrich yourself."

Janus Gallery

Fairmont Le Montreux Palace
Avenue Claude Nobs 2
Montreux
Tel 021 963 1884
info@janusgallery.com
www.janusgallery.com

There are art galleries and art galleries. Some are conventional and offer contemporary art, old masters or specific artists or periods. Others specialise in arts and crafts but Janus Gallery's tendency is to push outside the envelope. The owner,

Ilinca Vlad likes a challenge and to extend beyond the normal boundaries of what is considered art.

One of her past exhibitions was titled, Jean Cocteau, Sylvie Godel: A dreamlike dialogue. The French superstar meets the fragile ceramic artist in what Ilinca termed was similar to the Beauty and the Beast. The porcelain pieces of the young Swiss artist brought a delicate counterpoint, a naive freshness to the multitalented, voracious creative appetite of Cocteau. The exhibition took place 50 years after Cocteau's death when over 40 works covering the 1920's to the end of his life in 1963 were sold in Montreux.

"I'm thrilled with my exhibition on Zep," she said when she had Philippe Chappuis aka Zep, the Swiss comics creator of Titeuf in her gallery, "because I feel that comic art has been neglected. His reaction to my invitation went beyond all expectations. He came several times in Montreux prior to the opening and created original drawings not only of Montreux and its surroundings - the colourful crag of Rochers-de-Nayes and the bent and twisted branches of a tree which are my favourites but also scenes that include Titeuf next to the Freddie Mercury statue and the watercolour of him riding on the back of a swan. What made my day was when a little Malaysian boy came into the gallery and recognised Titeuf on the swan. His grandparents with him had known nothing about the comic character."

Ilinca Vlad who was born in Rumania, grew up in Vaud. She is the only child of parents who were both doctors - her father, Nicolas, was a gynaecologist and her mother, Manuela, a child psychiatrist. Ilinca became a lawyer at the suggestion of her parents but later followed her true vocation when she opened the Janus Gallery in 2012. She had two picture moments as a teenager. The first was on seeing Vermeer's Woman with the water jug at the Metropolitan Museum of Art in New York. The second was in the Scrovegni chapel, Padua where she saw the masterpieces of 14th century art - the complete series of frescos of Giotto in his maturity.

"I was fortunate with my parents as they had a great interest in art," she said. "My dad who was in love with the Impressionists took me to Paris to see them. My mother countered by making me aware of Byzantine art. On my own, I discovered applied art when I spent time in Noufaux,a village near Yverdon. Philip Baldwin and Monica Guggisberg who are artists of glass had a studio in a barn next door which I often visited. I could sit there for hours looking at them blowing glass. I was mesmerised, seeing this wonder repeat itself again and again: out of a furnace, a chunk of hot glass would be pulled and then worked until a transparent and colourful form would emerge. That was true magic. Then the creation of different shapes and forms."

One of her new projects is to organise an art competition on the theme of 'Death becomes her'. Her invitation to 150 contemporary jewellers consists of Anoush Abrar and Aimée Hoving's provocative photo of a blonde with an eye mask of orchids. Only 31 artworks will be kept for the exhibition. The original 'Death becomes her' was the title of a movie (1992) which starred Goldie Hawn, Meryl Streep, Bruce Willis and Isabella Rossellini. It was also the name of an exhibition curated by the Costume Institute at Metropolitan Museum of Art which displayed a century of mourning attire from 1815-1915.

Ilinca Vlad never forgot her initial encounter with Baldwin and Guggisberg and one evening in 2007, some 20 years later, she was on a vaporetto in Venice bound for Murano to take classes with the master glass craftsman Davide Penso. She has also proved her talent as a jewellery designer and gives a workshop on the subject at her gallery together with Hélène Othenin-Girard.

Ilinca is a warm and sparkling personality who is a refreshing presence on the Montreux art scene. She is fearless and her ability of crossing art boundaries will ensure that she will make a significant contribution in the future.

Plexus Art Gallery

Villa Murillo
Rue du Lac 61
1815 Montreux Clarens
Tel 079 241 8913/026 321 5435
info@galleryplexus.com
www.galleryplexus.com
www.plexus-events.com

The Plexus gallery which is run by Bernard Chassot is housed in the beautiful Murillo villa. It was designed by Eugene Jost, architect of Beau Rivage hotel, Ouchy and Caux Palace in 1897 and its name is derived from a mistress of a banker from Basel for whom it was built. She was thought to look like one of the women painted by Bartolomé Esteban Murillo (1617-1682). Such details attracted Bernard Chassot who is fascinated by the world of art.

"I was born with the idea of owning a gallery," he said, "and I took me some 20 years to realise the idea. I first ran an antique shop and started to exhibit paintings there. But it was not enough and I eventually opened my first gallery in Fribourg."

He came to Montreux in 2011 and opened a gallery at the Helvetia hotel and then found the Murillo villa. A couple, Pierre and Susy Bondolfi, who had renovated it but never moved in because the husband died. The widow was happy to rent it to him as a gallery provided he also lived there. He was chuffed as it was unthinkable that such a private place could be open to the public.

"My passion for art is such that I can't say no to artists who want to exhibit," he said. "It's important for me to find the right place for each artwork. The beauty of the villa's setting and the exquisite interior provides many opportunities for displaying paintings and sculptures. They have invaded the ground floor, the first floor and the garden and are even in the kitchen and bathroom. For me art expresses emotions and it's nice to see visitors' reactions to the

Bernard Chassot

contemporary art collection from all over the world. Peter Cerruti is a prize- winning medical researcher who interrupted his scientific career to become a figurative painter. Another example is José Roosevelt from Rio de Janeiro who is a self-taught surrealist painter. Martine Wehrel who trained at the Beaux-Arts and the Ecole de Louvre and a sculptress has also shown her work here."

Bernard Chassot also holds music and poetry recitals in villa Murillo. A visit to Plexus is a double pleasure because it is a personal invitation to a private sumptuous residence and at the same time, an emotive journey of contemporary artworks.

The Plexus Art gallery and the Fairmont Le Montreux Palace have together opened a gallery space devoted to Jean Miotte, a French abstract painter.

Shops

Confiserie Zurcher

Avenue du Casino 45
Montreux
Tel 021 963 5963
info@confiserie-zurcher.ch
www.confiserie-zurcher.ch

Open Tuesday to Sunday. 8 am to 6.30 pm Zurcher is an institution that reminds one of the famous confiserie and tearoom, Fortnum and Mason, Piccadilly, London. It's been in the centre of Montreux for over 130 years and you can enjoy lunch, coffee or tea with a yummy range of pastries.

Here, the mouth-watering selection of pralines, truffles and other specialities like the nougatine fish are made in a chocolate laboratory by artisans in the great tradition of Swiss chocolates. The way the chocolates melt on the tongue you can tell that they are not made in factories. They are also displayed in small presentation boxes like jewels. Anne Rapin-Zurcher is the fifth generation to run the establishment.
(See entry in People.)

Confiserie Zurcher

Roman Mayer

Av. du Casino 39
CH-1820 Montreux
Tel 021 963 3424
info@roman-mayer.ch
www.roman-mayer.ch

Silver Finger

"For me the most beautiful present is a client trusting us and going away happy and satisfied," said Josephine Christidis-Mayer. "It's important to offer something that suits them which could also be less expensive. We work for the future not for short term. In 1888 as well as today, the strength of Roman Mayer is the family spirit and the professionalism."
The prestigious jewellery shop Roman Mayer, Montreux was founded by Josephine Christidis-Mayer's grandfather. He emigrated to Switzerland from Pforzheim and his first business was located in the arcade under the Grand Hotel Territet. Among his noble clients was Sissi, the Empress Elizabeth of Austria whose favourite jewels were stars made of pearls and diamonds. Josephine's story really begins with her illustrious father Albert Mayer who was born in 1890 and took over the jewellery shop with his mother when his father, Roman, died in 1911.

"He was a multi-talented man," she said, "and very involved in the army, sports and politics. He was a good businessman, good soldier, good politician, good sportsman and above all, a good man. In 1908, he was given Swiss nationality and a year later, at 20 was drafted into the army and sent on an officers' course. In business, he continued and consolidated with his brothers and sisters his father's work at the various branches in Vulpera, St-Moritz, Zermatt and Interlaken. In 1922, he opened a new shop in Montreux near the Casino where the shop is today."

Josephine is the doyenne of the jewellery business and a talented designer. She studied gemology and is an active member of the Swiss Gemmology Society. She has made important pieces for clients. One of her favourites is an art deco clasp made of lapis lazuli for a five-strand pearl necklace. She was inspired when she went swimming and thought of the pearls as bubbles of water linked to the blue surface.

"When a client orders a special design, I tell them to come back in about three weeks," she explained. "That gives me time to think about them and be inspired. One request was for a birthday/wedding anniversary, the jewel had to have a porcelain piece, impossible to find on the market. Almost at the end of the second week, I suddenly had a brain wave. In my kitchen I had a porcelain charm which I had once received in La galette des Rois. I used this in the creation of a gold charm - a miniature pot with the inscription 'elixir of long life.' The client left the shop with a unique jewel.'"

Josephine has received strange requests in her time from eccentric clients. One was to make a silver urn for the ashes of a clients's mother. The ashes were not to be scattered in the countryside but kept in a silver box. She checked with an undertaker and discovered that they recommended an airtight box in which the cover folded

Family Christidis-Mayer: Stephanie, Petros, Alexandre and Josephine ©Chantal Dervey/24heures

inside and was sealed. Other commissions included replicas of lost pieces based on photographs, a three-piece body chain and a silver finger!

"One of the strangest orders I received was from a serious man about 30," she said. "It was an express order - to be completed in three days, for a gold chain necklace. Once we had sorted out the size, he also wanted a gold chain belt. But he had difficulty in describing the size of the waist. So I called my female staff who are different shapes and sizes and we stood in front of him. Finally, between us we were able to measure the size of the belt. His next request was very odd as he wanted a third gold chain to link the neck chain to the waist chain along her back. We were concerned as It would restrict her movement when she bent and hurt her neck. It was then that we found out that the three linked gold chains were called 'submission'. Another strange order was for a silver finger. A law student wanted a silver finger to slip onto his forefinger and it had to be slightly bent to carry more comfortably. It was to be engraved and open a bit so that the nail could be seen."

There is also another aspect of jewellery that requires intricate work. The transformation of watches and jewellery. When large watches became fashionable, a client brought in his Cartier and Bulgari alarm clocks to convert into wristwatches. The result were watches with diameters of 60 mm. Conversion of jewellery is also undertaken like changing a design of a tiger necklace in solid gold with tiger cubs, all of which have aquamarine eyes. She redesigns rings and necklaces by modernising settings as well as family heirlooms which are badly damaged or broken and gives them a new lease of life. "I was the only child and my father died when I was 12," she said. "He was a celebrated figure by then, nevertheless, he always spent a lot of precious moments with me. You can see in the photograph taken on my eighth birthday. When we went for a walk, he'd hold my hand in his pocket and we'd stop every 10 m to greet someone. My father achieved the rank of major and was the adjutant and friend of General Henri Guisan who was also from Vaud. He was a member of the International Olympic Committee, president of the Swiss Olympic committee and an active local politician as well as an MP for Canton Vaud. But above all, he was a jeweller par excellence and the brand Roman Mayer was known by an international clientele."

When Josephine grew up, she had not thought of following in her father's footsteps. She decided to study languages and now speaks eight. However, Arthur Schmidt, a cousin from Geneva offered her an apprenticeship in his jewellery shop. She accepted and soon found the work congenial. After five months she decided to apply at the Watchmaking Training Centre in Lausanne as a degree would be needed to run Roman Mayer in Montreux. In 1977, she graduated and at the age of 21 began her career in management and as a jewellery designer. In 1983, she married Petros Christidis who had done similar studies and joined the firm. Today, their son Alexandre who is interested in watchmaking and daughter, Stéphanie, who graduated as a gemmologist and jewellery designer work side by side with their parents.

Mad About Watches

Alexandre Christidis is the scion of the jewellery family Roman Mayer. He never considered working in the family business because he was interested in finance. Although, he was intelligent, he was never interested in studying. One day when his father was away for a few weeks, he offered to help his mother in the shop.

"I immediately felt at home and liked the ambiance," he said. "When my father returned I asked if I could work there. My parents agreed on one condition that I had to be punctual everyday. My hours were from 9 am to 6.30 pm. I started in the back office and gradually went into sales. I loved meeting people and watches became my passion. I liked the precision and unique temperament of each watch. Later, I gained my state diploma in watchmaking consultancy and worked with all brands. I developed a special relationship with Chopard, Omega and Patek Philippe which we had stocked since the 20th century."

Alexandre is proud of the Patek Philippe connection because he admires their approach to watchmaking. For example, they guarantee that they will repair any of their watches since their foundation in 1839. In some cases, it means that they have to resort to taking watches from their private museum collection - the largest in the world, to replicate parts. For him this is the epitome of after-sales service.

"One of my memorable moments was when a customer came into the shop and wanted to buy a Rolex," he said. "We don't stock the brand and I enquired whether I could show him another classical brand, Patek Philippe. He agreed and I explained that each watch is an art piece and can take anything from three months to three years to make. Also they have a long term investment because of the superb after-sales service and each watch has a sentimental value. An hour later he walked out with a Patek Philippe. What made the occasion memorable was that he thanked me because I'd convinced him."

Watches and cars are still an important status symbol for men, according to Alexandre. But when you're not in your car, people can see your watch. He himself has four watches. The first was a yellow one, a Paul Picot, which he admired and was given to him on his 18th birthday. Since then he has an Omega, Zenith and a Blancpain. What about a Patek Philippe? "I like too many models and take my time to choose the right one."

"The appearance of a watch can be deceptive," he warned. "You can have a watch studded with diamonds. But then again a simple looking watch with a minute repeater can be worth ten times more. It chimes the hours, the quarter hours and minutes. The number of components needed, the array of edges to be polished and the high level of skills required to put them all together mark them as haut de gamme watchmaking. The mechanism was invented by an English cleric, Edward Barlow in 1678."

He like his sister is happy to be part of a business which was started by his great grandfather in 1888 and enjoys working everyday.

Naked Without Diamonds

Stephanie Christidis-Mayer who is an attractive young woman likes diamonds and when she was five years old, she asked her father for diamond earrings. But her mother put a stop to that with the question, "If we give her diamonds at her age, what are we going to give her at 20? A diamond coronet?" But she was rewarded for her patience because she received a single diamond necklace on her 13th birthday.

"I was always in the jewellery shop during my school life," she said. "I was with my father in the morning when he opened up the shop before I went to school and then in the afternoon, I did my homework there. At home I was helping my mother who is a jewellery designer with her drawings. But I always dreamed of working with stones." When she finished school, she decided to study law in Fribourg. But it did not last long. Instead after an apprenticeship in Chopard, she did a course in gemmology at the Gemmology Institute of America in London. Established in 1931, it is the world's top non profit institution of gemmology research and education. Like her mother she likes the Art Deco jewellery and enjoys jewellery design.

"I find it magical that such beautiful stones like diamonds, emeralds, sapphires and rubies come from the earth," she said. "For me, jewellery enhances the beauty of women. I would feel naked if I didn't wear jewellery when I leave the house in the morning. The best place is on the hands."

Like her brother Alexandre, she is happy to follow the tradition of the Roman Mayer family.

Touzeau

Avenue du Casino 28
1820 Montreux
Tel 021 966 3010
monique@touzeau.com
www.touzeau.com

Rue du Rhone 65
Geneva
Tel 022 312 3666
www.touzeau.com

Place de l'Hôtel de Ville
Annemasse
+33 450 381389
www.touzeau.com

Moliere on the Scene

Monique Touzeau who is the president of the firm is a remarkable woman. She has a talent for the art of tableware and interior design at her fingertips which few can match in Switzerland. Her store is a palace of light with displays of beautiful household objects from tableware, crystal, silverware, china, furniture, carpets and things you never dreamt of.

"I like people to browse in my store," she said, " and they will be surprised at what they'll find. Quality does not always mean expensive. There are items to suit all pockets. Some customers confuse objects of great value which are rare and precious with a range of practical household objects. Our purchasing policy is to offer a range to suit everyone."
Monique Touzeau lives in Villeneuve and was born in Annemasse. Her parents ran a shop for bathroom and kitchen products

Beatrice Touzeau

Bruno Touzeau

Maurice and Monique Touzeau

and they instilled in her a passion for her job. They gradually spread into tableware and household objects. She liked the concept and when she met her husband, Maurice Touzeau, who was a well known chocolatier, she knew that his name would be ideal for a tableware shop. For a period, they operated two shops. Eventually the tableware prevailed over the chocolates. He joined her in the new venture and they have never looked back. Today, they have three shops - Geneva, Annemasse and Montreux and 30 employees.

"I'm shy by nature," she said, "and I allow time for a client to absorb the environment before addressing them. But then I come out of my shell and I am compelled by a desire to find the best thing for the person looking for a gift or wanting to buy something specific. After 30 years in the business, I have an inexhaustible knowledge and experience in tableware."

An enjoyable and fascinating experience is to be taken on a tour of her palace of light. You not only get a parade of the great names of silver (Christofle, Ercuis, Puiforcat, Alessi, Robbe & Berking, Odiot...), china (Rosenthal, Wedgwood, Villeroy & Boch, Hermes...), crystal (Baccarat, Daum, Lalique, St. Louis, Sevres ...), Limoges porcelain (Bernardaud, Haviland, Raynaud, Coquet ...) but also insights and stories about them.

"My favourite design period is Art Deco," she said. "René Lalique, the glass designer, was noted for his Art deco pieces and among other things designed the famous hood ornament of the Rolls Royce which was called 'Spirit of the Wind.' My daughter Beatrice who runs our shop in Geneva is responsible for the Lalique brand. Another company which is interesting is Christofle. It was founded in 1830 by the jeweller Charles Christofle who was prescient to buy licenses of electroplating. It is now in the hands of the fifth generation and one of its many outstanding pieces is a Cubist inspired Teacup and saucer designed by Louis Süe in 1927. Riedel which is run by the 11th generation offers wine glasses for different types of wine from Chardonnay and Pinot Noir to Riesling and Cabernet Sauvignon. With Daum, seven workers are needed to complete a decorative crystal piece!"

The wedding gift list is another service Touzeau offers. It is posted on internet and enables guests to see the items to purchase or to make comments.

"Our strength is that we are a family business," she said. "My daughter Beatrice runs the Geneva shop and my son, Bruno, the one in Annemasse and I yo-yo between France and Switzerland most of the time. My only regret is that I didn't have more children so I could open more Touzeau stores. There's no question about it but I'm sure I'll die on the scene like Moliere.

"From my childhood, I decided to follow my mother's vocation," said Beatrice Touzeau. "Lalique is my favourite because it's a special crystal with a texture of satin and is very sensual."

Boutique Sir Montreux

Rue du Quai 1
Montreux
Tel 021 963 2590
Info@sir-montreux.com
www.sir-montreux.com

Jermyn street in Montreux? Can you find bespoke tailoring and luxury items for men? The answer is yes, sir at Sir! Since 1964, the store has offered complete wardrobes for day and evening with a dash of Italian design like Ravazolo.

1

"We even can offer smoking jackets and suits," said Patrice Ducrot who lives in Territet, "with satin or silk lapels and if you want, a smoking suit with stripes down the trousers. But otherwise we specialise in high quality tailored suits such as Brioni, Canali among others and cloths from Dormeuil or the fourth generation Ermenegildo Zegna made-to-measure or couture collections."

Patrice Ducrot who was born in Paris has a diploma in textiles and worked for textile companies in France. He has managed Sir since 1987.

"You can't just categorise that bankers wear dark suits," he said. "There are important subtle differences. CEOs and directors tend to wear navy blue while other executives wear dark grey or black. What I enjoy most is to advise clients on their clothes. It's not a question of price but what suits them best."
Besides customised suits, Sir also has a range of Gant, Boss, Paul & Shark as well as shoes, underwear and other accessories

for a gentleman of fashion.

Bazar Suisse

Grand-Rue 24
CH-1820 Montreux
Tel 021 963 32 74
www.bazarsuisse.ch

Norbert Muller who lives in Montreux runs the Bazar Suisse. It's an Ali Baba's cave of souvenirs where you can find a vast selection of items. There are Victorinox Swiss Army knives; Cuckoo clocks - a range of 25; Figurines - from nativity scenes, Formula 1 drivers like Michael Schumacher, jazz and rock stars to Tintin statuettes; Early posters with various scenes from Montreux beach to Zermatt; Ravensburger puzzles of Chillon castle and Swiss maps; Swiss souvenirs from mugs, cows, key rings to snow globes and magnets;Toys from mini electric guitars to original Heidi Ott dolls. All these items are also available from the online shop, bazarsuisse.ch

But the pride of place is given to Queen and Freddie Mercury souvenirs. Norbert Muller has many official and exclusive items authorised by Queen Management Ltd. which can only be bought in his shop in Montreux. In the online shop, the most popular items which are available are the Freddie Mercury statuettes at CHF 69, the Freddie Mercury biography by Peter Freestone at CHF 35, as well as many other books or calendars. There are also nice posters at CHF 15 among other 40 items.
Norbert Muller besides being a fan of Freddie Mercury and Queen has organised for over 10 years together with Peter Freestone and Rita Balesi Grass the Freddie Mercury Montreux Memorial Day Weekend until 2011. He largely contributed to the website montreuxmusic.ch which is a godsend to fans as it has everything you need to know about Freddie Mercury/Queen or rock and jazz music in Montreux from the 1970s until now.

La Griffe Ausoni

Grand Rue 20 & 100
Montreux
Tel 021 963 8494
info@ausoni-montreux.ch
www.ausoni-montreux.ch

La Griffe Ausoni is fashion boutique with luxury brands such as Leonard, Philipp Plein, Max Mara, Armani, Versace, Roberto Cavalli, Brunello Cucinelli, Hogan and Gucci for men, women and children.

The business was started in 1906 by Eufonio Ausoni, an orphan who came from Livorno, Italy. Jean-Claude who was the third generation opened the Montreux boutique in 1969. The maxim is "The best is only good enough." It covers the high quality of the clothes and the service which also includes a workshop with seamstresses and tailors.

Maria Ausoni and her three sons, Frédéric, Marc and Philippe, the fourth generation, carry on the tradition. In 2010, another store was opened in the same street, some 40 years later. An icon of the shop in Montreux is the amazing collection of cat illustrations which have been created specially by Etienne Delessert, a famous Swiss graphic artist and illustrator.

Maria Ausoni goes to the fashion shows in Paris, Dusseldorf and Zurich to choose designers she likes. One of the discoveries was Zuhair Murad, a Beirut based designer.

"Fashion evolves slowly," she said, " but one must be open to the world and adapt the clients to the new trends. I myself and the experienced staff of 11 are there to assist them."

Cardis SA

Rue du Theatre 7bis
Montreux
Tel 021 962 8662
montreux@cardis.ch
www.cardis-sothebysrealty.ch

Thomas Geiser is director of the Cardis estate agency. It is part of Sothebys international realty network which specialises in luxury property as well as other properties of quality. The agency covers the whole of the French-speaking region.

"The big advantage of the Montreux Riviera is that you have everything on your doorstep," he said. "The location is central. A hour from Geneva and two from Zurich. For newcomers, there is a good selection of schools and a safe environment for children who can play outside their homes. One of the big benefits are sport activities because the location is between the Alps and Lake Geneva. You can ski in resorts of les Pacots, Leysin, les Diablerets, Villars or les Portes du Soleil which is one or the largest ski areas in the world in about 30 minutes in less than an hour in Verbier or Crans-Montana. In summer, there are water sports on the lake like rowing, swimming and boating. For the rest, there are famous clinics like La Prairie and the climate is mild all the year round and supports palm trees and other exotic plants."

1

Thomas Geiser knows the Montreux Riviera well as he was educated there. He also has experience of dealing with many cultures during his career with the SBB.

"Each nationality has its own property requirement," said Geiser. "The Russians want the best places - the most central location, the nicest view and high ceilings. Middle East clients also like to be in the centre and like the rainy weather. The French want a quiet location with no roads, no trains and as cheap as possible. The Germans appreciate the climate and dislike mist and grey weather. They like the fact that Switzerland is well organised and clean. The English want a view and like to be near a ski area. They also want to make a good investment."

There is a difference in buying homes in Switzerland compared to the UK. Here the buyers never own the property outright. They make a down payment of 20% (or 30-35% in the case of foreigners) to the bank and are in debt for the rest of their life. The reason for this is a tax advantage. Whereas in the UK it is important to own the house and they can benefit with each increase in price. Luxury apartments in the Montreux area sell for 8,000 to 12,000 Swiss francs per square metre and at the higher-end can reach 15,000 to 25,000 Swiss francs a square metre if the location has a spectacular and unobstructed view.

"We have all sorts of properties on our books," he said. "One was a two-bedroom two-bath penthouse apartment in Chernex overlooking Montreux on Lake Geneva for 3.2 million Swiss francs. The Venetian stone floor tiles in the living room were heated. Currently, we have a 6.5 room triplex apartment in Montreux with 240 m2 of living area for 3.95 million Swiss francs. It is situated in the highest tower of a beautiful 19th century building in the city centre and has a double garage, a cellar, and a panoramic 306 degree view of lake and Alps."

Geiser is proud of the one-stop service he can offer clients from millionaires to people on salaries. He is really fortunate as the region he represents is one of the most beautiful in Switzerland.

Hotel Victoria

Hotels and Restaurants

Hotel Victoria

1823 Clion-sur-Montreux
021 9628282
info@victoria-glion.ch
www.victoria-glion.ch

Hotelier Extraordinaire

To stay at the Victoria hotel is truly a unique experience. The idyllic surroundings, the quiet Gentleman's Club atmosphere and the discrete service of the dedicated staff make it a memorable experience.

The Victoria hotel which is a prominent landmark in Glion above Montreux, started out as a modest establishment in 1869. It is the very panorama that inspired Jean-Jacques Rousseau's novel The New Heloise. The hotel has had five owners and each time the hotel was extended. As a result, it ended up with magnificent lounges and a veranda. Views from the balconies of the rooms are stunning as it shows the lake Geneva in all its glory in the different seasons and hours of the day.

It is little wonder that over the decades it has attracted the great and the good. In the 1920's, the German poet Rainer Maria Rilke used the Victoria hotel as the pleasurable extension of the Valmont clinic whenever he had treatment there. Other notables followed suit: the artist Oskar Kokoschka; singers like Joan Sutherland and Charles Aznavour; kings and religious leaders like Albert Paolo of Belgium, the Shah of Persia and the Aga

1

Toni Mitermair and guests

Khan; the writer Simenon; the dancer from Diaghalev's Ballet Russe, Serge Lifar; film stars Kirk Douglas and James Mason; the cellist Rostropovich; and top chef Paul Bocuse and the confiserie family of the Sprünglis.

Toni Mittermair who is a hotelier extraordinaire has run the Victoria for the past four decades. He has made significant contributions to the art collection and the cuisine. The hotel is furnished in the Belle Epoque style and he has added over 500 artworks including Art Nouveau and Vienna Secession objects like the charming bronze of Mozart playing the violin. The cuisine is inspired by the south of France and one of the specialities is ribs of Sisteron lamb with herbs, straw potatoes and ratatouille.

"I came to the Victoria in 1966 as chef de cuisine to work for a season" he said, "and have stayed ever since. My father was a butcher and ran an inn near Lake Constance and after gaining a diploma at the hospitality school, I worked at La Grappe d'or, Lausanne for two years. I travelled to England, Spain, Paris and Austria and on my return, I got the job at the Victoria which I liked very much. But after three years, when business had tailed off, I decided to leave. The owner Roger Lazzarelli induced me to stay when he offered me the position of manager."

The 4-star hotel has an old-fashioned charm with a large garden, an outdoor swimming pool, a tennis court and a golf practice area. Guests can also enjoy the sauna, massages and fitness area. The decoration in each bedroom is individualised with white, pink and blue interiors and interspersed with valuable antiques.

"Guests don't book-in or come to a hotel," he said, "they come to our home. I'm assisted by my wife Barbara and we both have a desire to satisfy each guest. I have been a member of the Relais & Chateaux since 1975. In keeping with the association, our luxury hotel and restaurant has a distinctive character. I am proud that some 90% of our guests eat regularly in our restaurant."

Grand Hotel Suisse Majestic

Avenue des Alps 45
1820 Montreux
Tel 021 966 3333
hotel@suisse-majestic.ch
www.suisse-majestic.com

General Patton

Grand Hotel Suisse Majestic was built during the Belle Epoque in 1870 and was thoroughly renovated in 2010 at a cost of CHF 25 million. The hotel is a 4-star deluxe with 155 rooms. The hotel is centrally located opposite the train station, near the Congress centre, casino and shops. The restaurant 45 has one of the best panoramas of the lake and mountains in Montreux. It is also distinguished for its hard wood floors. The general manager, Andrés Oppenheim, is a charismatic figure and in conversation is likely to come up with quotes from Napoleon, General George Patton and Pope John Paul I.

"When I was appointed to run the hotel,"

Grand Hotel Suisse Majestic

said Andrés Oppenheim, "the property was like a patient on oxygen who needed to be revived otherwise it would die. But by 2009, I had tripled the room nights and by 2014, it had quadrupled."

He studied hospitality both in Germany and in Switzerland. He was an apprentice chef for three years at Steigenberger hotels and resorts and was awarded a prize for the best apprentice in Germany. He completed his hospitality studies in the Lausanne Hospitality School and his first position was at the Beau Rivage in Lausanne.

"What I would like my guests to have is an experience at the hotel," he said. "It's not just a place to eat and sleep. In summer, we open the terrace and we have live music almost every night. A special feature is the saxophonist who plays smooth stuff in the early evening hours. It's not a boring place, there's always something happening. The big thing about Montreux Riviera is that you have Switzerland in a nutshell on the doorstep within 30-45 minutes."

Oppenheim believes that the role of general manager is analogous to that of a captain of a ship. He gives orders and the staff are expected to follow them. Of course, a good captain allows officers to question and challenge him. But never to argue with him, particularly during a storm. He cites the case of a restaurant manager who in the second day of the high season got into a disagreement with him and would not back down. So he fired him in spite of the problem it would cause. He doesn't have a sales director as he feels that the loyal and honest officers on the ship can manage without him when he travels abroad to promote the hotel.

"I'm only as good as my team," he said. "I create an enthusiastic atmosphere around me by employing young people with a keenness to learn rather than those who are better qualified. I myself was once given responsibility far beyond my years and experience. My mentor, Willy Brawand of Ciga hotels told me, 'Just do it and if you do your best, there's little chance that you'll make a mistake. But if you mess up, I'll sort it out.' I use the same policy with my staff.'"

Oppenheim is one of the most successful general managers on the Montreux Riviera. His role model is General Patton who inspired confidence in his men and in return got their total loyalty. He egged on his men with the command, "We shall attack and attack until we are exhausted and then we shall attack again." A most remarkable achievement was when the tanks and infantry of the Third army roared across six European countries in 10 months. Napoleon too was a good example to Oppenheim during the battle of Austerlitz. Although, he was outnumbered, he won a brilliant victory. It was a tactical masterpiece and comparable to the ancient battle of Cannae. To cap the examples he quotes Pope John Paul II who said, "Never be afraid."

In the meantime, when Oppenheim is not on deck at the hotel, he is chasing MICE on his travels. The acronym represents meetings, incentives, conferences, events. It's little wonder that he has the highest occupancy rates in Montreux. That is to be expected from a hotelier extraordinaire.

Fairmont Le Montreux Palace

Avenue Claude Nobs 2
Tel 021 9621212
montreux@fairmont.com
www.montreux-palace.ch

Nabokov's Place

Today in a crowded world, space is at a premium and there is a tendency to downsize. However, at the Fairmont Le Montreux Palace you can luxuriate in spaciousness. Treat yourself!

If you come to the Montreux Riviera, there are only two buildings of note to

Salle des Fêtes

see. One is Chillon Castle which most people know about and the other is the Fairmont Le Montreux Palace. The luxury 5-star hotel is a stupendous place with a grandeur and spaciousness which would put a British Duke or two totally at ease. If you have been to Blenheim Palace where Churchill was born you will know what is meant. Most people are unaware that this treasure is also protected as a Swiss national monument like Chillon Castle. And imagine there are 15 conference rooms to entertain in! Three restaurants to choose from including La Terrasse Petit Palais which is open during summer and Montreux Jazz Cafe. Lastly, there is the Willow Stream Spa with two swimming pools, steam zones, treatment and fitness rooms. So it's easy to make a whole day of it or spent a couple of nights in total luxury. But don't leave Montreux without visiting the Palace.

"We hosted the Syrian peace talks in which two dozen foreign ministers including the US Secretary of State, John Kerry participated in January 2014," said Michael Smithuis, the General Manager. "But then it's not unusual because in 2010, the 13th summit of French speaking nations, La Francophonie, was held here and 30 heads of state including French President Nicolas Sarkozy stayed at the hotel. There's a plaque on the Salles des Fêtes to mark the event."

The luxury hotel has a total of 236 rooms with 51 suites including the three suites on the roof at the 7th floor. The major suite is the Quincy Jones with a bedroom and a separate living room, two terraces with views of the lake and Alps and a marble bathroom with a jacuzzi. For aficionados of jazz, there is a DVD set of all Quincy's recordings which can be heard on a Bang & Olufsen stereo system. For the politicos, there is a presidential suite and for Vladimir Nabokov fans there is a small suite in the Cygne wing with original furniture including his desk, lounge chairs and twin beds. He stayed there with his wife Vera for 16 years and preferred to entertain guests in the Salon de Musique.

"Today, the main focus is on conferences," said Michael Smithuis. "Some 60-65% of our business is done on banqueting and meetings. Besides the Belle Epoque function rooms, we can offer a totally modern function room with contemporary decor at the Petit Palais. This was where the Syrian peace talks were held."

The Swiss architect Eugene Jost built the Palace in 1906 and joined it to the Cygne hotel in 1906 via the Salon de Musique, the Grand Hall and richly decorated ballrooms. A Sports Hall was added in 1911 and guests came from all over the world: European aristocrats, Russian princes, New York bankers, maharajahs, among others.

"What most people do not realise is that it was long journey in that time to come to Montreux," said Gisele Sommer, PR Coordinator of the Fairmont Le Montreux Palace, " and when they arrived they expected to be entertained. There was ballroom dancing, a bridge salon, a theatre, billiard room, restaurants, a tea room and bars. In the Sports Hall, a shooting range, a skating and roller skating rink. Another unknown fact is that our corridors are extremely wide because they had to accommodate women passing each other dressed in bustles."

Tralala Hotel

Rue du Temple 2
1820 Montreux
Tel 021 963 4973
www.tralalahotel.ch
Vevey Hotel & Guesthouse
Tel 021 922 35 32

Nothing Just Happens

Estelle Mayer who has the sultry looks of a French film star is the dynamic owner of the boutique hotel Tralala. She is the third generation in hospitality. Her grandparents ran restaurants in Montreux, Villars and les Diablerets and she grew up in her parents' restaurant, Apollo in Montreux. The hotel Tralala has 35 bedrooms and suites and a conference room. It's themed with music which Montreux is famous for through the Jazz and September Festivals. Each room is unique and is dedicated to an artist who contributed to Montreux's reputation. So you have a choice of David Bowie, Aretha Frannklin, Miles Davis, ZZ Top, Santana and even to be inspired by Igor Stravinsky who composed The Rites of Spring (1912) and on his lakeshore walks, gave rise to Petroushka.

The building which is located in the picturesque old town of Montreux dates back to 1616 and was renovated in 2008. The interior design is cool. Estelle is to be congratulated because she carried everything out herself and combined the modern black and white colours with the warmth of the deep, rich purple. You find Philippe Starck-like touches such as the white egg chair with crimson interior contrasted with the crimson egg cup canopy with the white interior. The black

Estelle Mayer

and white reception area with the black ceiling is a knockout as well as the black and white portraits of musicians painted on the walls of the rooms.

"My dream was always to have a B&B and one day I drove past this place with my husband, Nicolas," she said, " and I knew this was it. So we bought the building and turned it into accommodation we'd like to stay in when we travel. I wanted a small, modern place but still warm and with a soul. It also had to be an amazing and a relaxing hotel with bedrooms - similar to those which friends who would offer you in their attic, without breaking the bank. A 3-star hotel, a category of hotels which is lacking according to Chsitoph Sturny of the Tourist office."

Although, Estelle's background is hospitality, she has an interesting work history which shows her multi-talented personality. She ran a nightclub called Backstage with her brother Sven and worked in PR and Marketing for big corporations such as Philip Morris and British American Tobacco. She is also the owner of the Vevey hotel and guesthouse which is a hostel for backpackers. Then she took time off as a mother to bring up two children. But little matches her enthusiasm for Montreux which is in the heart of the Swiss Riviera. It's something that she has managed to pass on to her guests.

"I'm very happy that the hotel works well," she said. "We have an occupancy rate of about 75% and without a restaurant - we can provide snacks, the profitability of the business with a staff of ten is good. I've introduced afterwork parties on the first Thursday of the month which have become very popular."

She is the new president of the Société des Hôteliers Montreux Vevey Riviera (SHMV). The society represents 50 establishments with 2,000 rooms and employs some 2,000 people. There is a host of issues to deal with from the development of business, wine and third world tourism (China, India and Brazil) to major projects of the Nestlé Heritage centre and the Chaplin Museum which would attract future leisure travellers.

“It’s a little intimidating in such an environment where hotels are mostly run by men,” said Estelle. “But they’re the ones who proposed me and encouraged me to take the helm of the society. I trust that they will help and support me in this task.” I am sure that Estelle Mayer will succeed brilliantly because she has a solid reputation of being a dynamic entrepreneur. Her philosophy is simple. “Nothing just happens. You have to work, work, work. Life is beautiful, enjoy it all.”

Hotel Splendid

Grand rue 52 Montreux
Tel 021 966 7979
info@hotel-splendid.ch
www.hotel-splendid.ch

There are family run hotels and family run hotels. Some give lip service to the clients and offer comfortable environments but draw the line at going the extra mile. But Yvan Hausmann enjoys meeting people and forms friendships with his guests.

“I inherited this trait from my father, Peter, who on Valentine’s day would give all women he met in the hotel and restaurant a flower,” said Yvan. “It’s a good tradition which is still carried on today.”

Yvan who runs the hotel with his brother Grégoire, studied hotel management and took over the 3-star hotel in 2001. It is located centrally with 28 rooms which have lakeside views. He counts as mentors, Toni Mittermair of the Victoria hotel, Glion and Claude Nobs for whom he once worked and taught him how to receive people.

“One of the main attractions of the resort are the beautiful sunsets you can see from our rooms,” he said. “I’ve travelled a lot and the only comparable sunset I’ve seen is in Key West, Florida.”

Yvan has a commitment to sustainable development. He has changed all his lighting to LED light bulbs because of the greater energy efficiency in the hotel and lowered water and detergent consumption through the installation of computer controlled industrial washing machines. To top it all, he drives a battery operated vehicle.

Hotel Masson

Rue Bonivard 5
Veytaux-Chillon
CH-1820
Tel 021 966 0044
hotelmasson@bluewin.ch
www.hotel masson.ch

Hotel Masson which is one of the historic Swiss hotels is the oldest in Montreux-Vevey area. It has been renovated on several occasions and guests can enjoy the various authentic features: the 1875 wrought-iron balcony, the oak floorboards, the opulent granite staircase, the original furniture including the Viennese chairs in the dining room, the collection of paintings and the 1906 plaster mouldings.

The hotel is surrounded by a large garden with century-old trees in a quiet area and overlooks lake Geneva. It has a small spa with a sauna and a hot tub. The 31 bedrooms are decorated in the same style as the public areas with floral wallpaper and fabrics and have tiled bathrooms, cable tv, minibars and WiFi is available throughout the hotel. There is free parking on site and Chillon Castle is close by.

The family hotel is run by the second generation, Mr and Mrs Phlippe Sèvegrand. They took over from Mrs Anne-Marie Sèvegrand's parents, René and Jeanne Jacquier who bought the hotel in 1947. The Sèvegrand are proud of their market-fresh cuisine and homemade bread and jam served with a nice buffet breakfast.

Le Palais Oriental

Quai Ernest Ansermet 6
Montreux
Tel 021 963 1271
info@palaisoriental.ch
www.palaisoriental.ch

Montreux has interesting architecture from the old winemaker's houses and the Belle Epoque hotels to the modern skyscrapers of the sixties. But no building is more remarkable than the Oriental Palace. It is a masterpiece of Moroccan and Iranian architecture in the centre of Montreux and the second most photographed building in the riviera after Chillon Castle.

The Oriental Palace is cornucopia of authentic and tasty dishes from Iran, Lebanon and Morocco. It is a place to dine daily and each meal consists of a different cuisine. And of course, there is the finest caviar from Iran. But above all, the site is one of the most beautiful on the Montreux promenade and the view of the sunset is spectacular.

"When I took over the Oriental Palace in 1988," said Shahriar Gharibi who is the owner, "it was in disrepair. I renovated the building and where cornices were an austere white, I added colour. Later, I built a wooden veranda in the same style. But I was ready for a challenge as I had managed the Maison de l'Iran in Paris before. I am pleased that visitors appreciate the originality of the building."

The Oriental Palace which has been a private residence for decades, has the appearance of the Alhambra with ornate mosaics, exquisite marquetry and stained glass windows. It was built in 1896 as a residence for Count Puget and his sister had a smaller house next door. In the 1960s, it became the home of Mr Ahmad Belroul, a member of National Liberation Front of Algeria (FLN), who converted it into a Moorish style villa.

"I was born in Hashtjin, a village in north Iran and studied hospitality," Gharibi said. "I left Iran after the revolution. How I came to Switzerland is a fascinating story. I ran a restaurant at the ski resort, Shemshak, high in the Alborz mountains from 1974-81. It's located at 3,300m and is open five months of the year. One day, Swiss diplomats came to ski and they stayed longer than expected because temperatures dropped to -35 degrees C. And that's how I met my future wife, Therese."

They have a daughter Roseline who is

Le Palais Orientale

studying business administration at the University of St Gallen and she is a Swiss-Iranian beauty.

Gharibi is a self-made man and has turned the Oriental Palace which is a famous restaurant into a cultural centre. There are three floors. On the first is an art gallery of contemporary artists from the Middle East, Kazakstan, Turkey, Morocco, Iran and the UAE. On the second is another gallery with fine carpets. Some of the Persian carpets on display are exquisite and are artworks in themselves because of the creative designs and colour patterns.

"Hospitality in Europe requires the owner always to be visible," he said. "Consequently, you don't have a private life. My advice to your enemy is to tell him to have a restaurant. Otherwise, for those starting off in life, I would recommend that they have patience, are hardworking, never borrow money because that's a negative start, be modest, respect others and above all, have good relations with people - one hand washes another!"

Hotel Victoria Restaurant

1823 Glion-sur-Montreux
021 9628282
info@victoria-glion.ch
www.victoria-glion.ch

Each visit is a delight and when one leaves the table, you are accompanied by the thought of an early return.
The restaurant is one of the best kept secrets in Canton Vaud and even the inspectors from the top guide books are unaware of it otherwise it would have been showered with stars and 20 points. However, Toni Mittermair, the owner, has the best accolade already from the guests of the hotel as over 90% of them eat regularly in the restaurant during their stay.

The grand cuisine is exceptional and is complimented by the elegant ambiance and excellent service. Toni Mittermair is a restauranteur par excellence who started his career as a chef and throughout his life has devoted himself to the pleasures of the palate. He is a hands-on hotelier who personally selects the vegetables, the cheeses, the meat and the fish. So you can expect the best quality from his kitchen.

The menus are extraordinary with a wide choice to suit many tastes. There are three kinds: the plat de jour, the gourmand and à la carte which is embellished with a painting by Ed Menta (1882) from Toni's collection.

Dishes which are popular and are specially recommended: Starters of mille-feuille (Napoleon) of artichokes and goose liver with nut oil and Shell fish soup with Armagnac; Main courses of rack of lamb from Sisteron which is served with potatoes gallette and ratatouille niçoise; calf's kidneys with pilaf rice; Atlantic sole meunière and emincé of veal served with fresh mushrooms and Bernese rösti. The dessert is a soufflé with mandarin and Grand Marnier.

The wine list has great vintages and pleasant surprises from the best vineyards worldwide. Again the cover is decorated by a painting of Jules Chéret (1836-1932), from Toni's collection. (The artist became known as the master of the Belle Epoque poster art and father of the modern poster.) The stars from the list of reds include the Pomerol, Chateau Pétrus (1985), Chateau Margaux (1998) and Saint-Emilion, Cheval Blanc (1993). Among the whites the stars include the Batard-Montrachet Grand cru (2008); the Bordeaux Chateau D'Yquem Lur Saluces (1999); and the Bourgognes Richebourg Givrot (2000, 2002).

For the rest, the list extends from the Swiss red and whites to Italian wines like Barolo Fratelli Revello (2008), the Napa valley to Spain and Graham's vintage Port as well as Beaujolais and Valley of the Rhone.

La Rouvenaz Restaurant and hotel

Rue de Marché 1
Montreux
Tel 021 963 2736
rouvenaz@bluewin.ch,
hotel@rouvenaz.ch
www.rouvenaz.ch

Rouvenaz is a traditional restaurant which specialises in Italian cuisine and seafood. It has warm ambiance, a cool crowd and a good friendly service. Of special interest is the plat du jour which changes daily and is good value. There is wide choice of starters specially the fritto misto and bruschetta classica.

The fresh pasta is made in the traditional Italian way from the simple spaghetti with tomato and basil to seafood as well as tagliatelle with salmon candied lemon, vodka and fresh dill. The restaurant which is also known for its pizza and one of the most popular is the Montreux Grand Prix pizza, which pays tribute to the owner Ezio Vialmin who is the president of the Grand Prix.

There is also a good selection of main courses and among the popular dishes are grilled Sea Bass filet and mixed grill of fish. The house speciality for desserts are Tiramisu and nutella pizza dolce.
The hotel which is next door to the restaurant is in a good location and only 20 metres from the lake shore. Around the corner is Ezio Vialmin's ice cream shop Bellamia. The products which are made from organic ingredients, come in a feast of flavours.

Le Metropole

Restaurant and Bar
Grand-Rue 55-57 Montreux
Tel 021 9637558

The Montreux Riviera has always attracted famous Russian visitors from writers like Leo Tolstoy, Nicolas Gogol, Fyodor Dostoevsky,Vladimir Nabokov to musicians such as Tchaikovsky, Igor Stravinsky and Serge Diaghilev, founder of Ballet Russe.

Natalia Yudochkina, the owner of the Metropole, fell in love with Montreux when she came on holiday with her parents. Later, she was sent to the boarding school, Brilliantmont, Lausanne. She had never thought of career in hospitality despite the fact that her father owned a chain of restaurants.

"I'm a Swiss entrepreneur, born in Moscow and educated in Switzerland," said Natalia Yudochkina who is the youngest restaurateur in Montreux. "Like Nabokov, Montreux is my home and like Stravinsky I have been inspired by the place. In fact it had a great influence on my life. I wanted to study law but it meant that I had to go to Lugano. But I didn't want to leave Montreux so instead I decided on hospitality."

She studied for a Bachelor in Business Administration at the Hotel Institute Montreux (HIM). After her diploma, she gained a MBA at Glion, Institute of Higher Education in 2008. Her dissertation examined the differences between men and women entrepreneurs.

"While I was there, students would hang out at the Mayfair House. The bar and restaurant was across the road from the Metropole. One day, I heard that the owner wanted to sell the property. I was excited as the Metropole had a prime and strategic location."

Natalia began negotiations with the widow who owned the property and wanted to retire. The negotiations were prolonged - it took five years! There were all sorts of issues, for example, the owner did not want to turn the place into a fast food restaurant. In 2010, she bought the Metropole and was ready to put her theory into practice.

"Although, the Metropole had a good potential," she said, "I knew the business could be better exploited. I felt that I could make a success of my first business venture. It has taken four years to get the right staff and the appropriate menu. I'm proud of the positive responses from customers. In TripAdvisor, well travelled Americans commented 'the food was great and we had a very helpful waitress...' A couple from England commented,'Decent meal with a view.'"

With such a good start, one can certainly expect surprising things from the young entrepreneur. After all, Montreux is an inspiring resort.
The Metropole is a restaurant with a terrace overlooking lake Geneva in Montreux where you can have wholesome food with a beautiful view. What more does a visitor or local want. The location is just the opposite the landing of the CGN and you have a chance to view the Belle Epoque lake steamers and in winter the Christmas market.

The brasserie menu varies from starters like squid, chicken soup with shitake mushrooms and steak tartare to a nice selection of salads including Greek, Caesar and Niçoise. There's also a large range of pizzas with specialities like pepperoni pizza with arugula and cheese as well as bressola pizza. The main courses include perche from the lake and veal sausages. The desserts include the chef's special crepe suzette, creme brulée and a strawberry soup.
A special feature is freshly pressed juices including carrot which is served with cream that enables the vitamin D to be absorbed quickly. The staff are friendly and provide an efficient service.

The Metropole also comprises a bar and a banqueting space on the first floor with a view on the lake.

Montreux Jazz Cafe

Claude Nobs Avenue 2
At the Fairmont Le Montreux Palace Hotel
Montreux

The visit to the Cafe is a 'must' when you come to Montreux. It pays homage to Claude Nobs, founder of the Montreux Jazz Festival, and has an incredible collection of memorabilia as well as presents kindly loaned by his partner, Thierry Amsallem. The sublime white kimono which Freddie Mercury gave to Claude has pride of place. Also on display is the treasured loom given by Nesuhi Ertegun of Atlantic Records. "Every item, even the smallest has a history," said Mathieu Jaton, CEO of the festival, "and gives a better understanding of the man."

Claude Nobs was a passionate collector from trains to Tintin figurines and, of course, musical items like jukeboxes, radios and recorders. The walls of the restaurant are lined with 110 photos of half a century of musical history and heritage. Santana, Keith Jarrett and Herbie Hancock are among the many artists featured.

The highlight for diners is that they can see performers and hear their music on the television screens from the past live concerts. There is also a bar, Funky Claude's bar, for clients who like to listen to jazz over a drink.

The idea of the cafes originated from Claude Nobs and Quincy Jones who wanted to have a backstage cafe. Laurent Buri, COO of the franchise for the Montreux Jazz Cafes worldwide, went to his first concert at 16 to hear David Bowie in 1996.

"It was awesome and I never missed a concert since," he said, "except for the two years when I managed a hotel in Madagascar."
"This is more than a restaurant," said Michael Smithuis, General Manager of the Fairmont Le Montreux Palace, "it's more like an embassy of the festival which is open every day of the year."

Lucien Barrière Casino

Rue du Theatre 9
Tel 021 962 8383
www.casinodemontreux.ch

King of Swiss Casinos

Gilles Meillet who runs the Casino Barrière in Montreux was born in France at La Ferte-sous-Jouarre. His father was a farmer who produced veal and his ambition when he grew up was to be a chef. Instead he became the king of Swiss Casinos. But to achieve the goal, he was a perfectionist and always had fun. During the early years, he worked in Canada at Digby which was the capital of Nova Scotia. There he dined on lobsters and scallops which were cheaper than eating hamburgers.

"I was the first to establish a Grand casino in the French part of Switzerland," he said. "In 2001, I obtained a unrestricted A license. Within five years Montreux ranked as the top of all Swiss casinos. It took everyone by surprise even the Barrière group management. The staff were proud because it was a victory for the small over the large establishments."

Gilles Meillet was a good scholar and obtained a BA at the Thonon school of hospitality and attended several marketing courses including the University of Nevada. It took several years before he found his true vocation in casinos.

"I started work as a chef," he said, "but then realised that I would never be in the top echelon so I concentrated on F & B. I worked as a barman, waiter and even changed jobs every six months when I'd got everything from a place. This took me to Luxembourg, Paris and Canada. My big break came in 1985 when I joined Barrière hotels and casinos in France. I started on the hotel side and when I reached the top, I was offered a General Manager job of a hotel or a casino. I took the latter as it was more fun. It's easy to fill up hotel but a lot more difficult to fill up a casino. It was a big challenge which I enjoyed because mostly it's about marketing."

The first casino he was appointed General Manager was the Grand Deauville casino which was built in 1912 and was located on the town's famous boardwalk. It welcomed celebrities worldwide and played host to elegant and fashionable celebrations. Its sumptuous interior decor includes expanses of marble and columns and borders of gold and crimson.

"When I first came to Switzerland I fitted in well with life," he said. "The people are free and easy and honest and are decisive. It's either black or white and no grey which I like. The Swiss are also strict about gambling and they allow no credit to be given by casinos. They also have a strict control over gambling addiction."

The Montreux casino was completed in 10 months and was opened in February, 2003. It had a selection of slot machines and gaming tables. There were two types of gamblers those who came during the weekend who come in groups to party, to have fun and blow their money. Those during the week, tend to be single and prefer to have gains rather than the jackpot.

Haut-Lac International Bilingual School

Education

Switzerland is universally renowned for the quality and level of teaching to be found in its schools. There is a good choice of school serving the international community in Montreux Riviera. It varies from the primary level such as the day school International School Monts-de-Corsier, the Surval Montreux boarding school for young girls and the eminent Monte Rosa Institute for Junior and High school to Haut-Lac International Bilingual School in St- Legier which offers both primary and secondary curriculums. The region has a claim to have the best hotel schools such as Glion Institute of Higher Education and Swiss Education Group with the Hotel Institute Montreux (HIM) and the Swiss Hotel Management School (SHMS). (See entry Florent Rondez). There is also the prestigious Europe University, the business school.(See entry, Dr Dirk Craen)

Haut-Lac International Bilingual School

Chemin de Pangires 26
1806 St-Légier
Tel 021 555 5000
info@haut-lac.ch
www.haut-lac.ch

Eco-Friendly Campus

Haut-Lac International Bilingual School has been successfully educating both local and expatriate children since it was established in Vevey with just a few primary students in 1993. One of the leading private schools on the Riviera with

Jean-Louis & Grainne Dubler, Anne-Marie & Neil Harwood

an enrolment of 650 boys and girls aged 3-18 years representing 45 nationalities, it continues to maintain the family atmosphere encouraged by founders Anne-Marie and Neil Harwood and Grainne and Jean-Louis Dubler who remain at the helm.

The promotion of intercultural understanding and bilingualism and the preparation of well- informed, compassionate and responsible young adults are at the forefront of the educational philosophy practiced by the founders and their dedicated staff. The students' academic progress is shaped by the International Baccalaureate Learner Profile – Haut- Lac has been authorised to offer the IB Middle Years and Diploma Programmes since 2002. The IB Diploma results have been consistently high, leading to interesting and varied university and career choices.

In the infant and primary school, classes are taught in English and French on alternate days while in the secondary school most subjects can be studied in either language.

"Haut-Lac prides itself in being a true

1

bilingual school," said Jean-Louis Dubler, Managing Director, "It's good to start with languages at an early age as it is widely known that young children tend to be the most receptive." A multi-lingual teaching staff with backgrounds in both the Anglophone (UK, USA) and French-speaking (Belgium, Canada, France and Switzerland) educational systems ensures that this aim can be fulfilled.

Another aspect of the school's mission is the provision of learning experiences that are relevant to the 21st century. In this context, the use of new technologies (interactive whiteboards, 3D printers, robots, laser cutters) is integrated into teaching processes. Furthermore, the Haute Ecole Pédagogique in Lausanne is collaborating with Haut-Lac on a training and research project which will ensure the smooth introduction of 1:1 iPads in the upper primary classes.

Extracurricular experiences of the students are important alongside the academic education. "The school strives to offer a holistic education that helps children to grow as unique and talented individuals," said Neil Harwood. "Pupils are encouraged to take on not only sports and the arts, but also many other recreational activities."

Anne-Marie Harwood commented further: "In addition, to forming well-rounded individuals such activities can improve young people's self-assurance, promote their interaction with others outside of school and help them perform better overall." This includes stimulating The awareness of issues in the world around them is stimulated and gives them the confidence to become actively involved.

A new eco-friendly campus in St-Légier was completed in 2014. It includes a triple gym and a large hall with stage that doubles as the school dining room and has opened new horizons for the future development of Haut-Lac.

"The building is on four floors and inspires children to be curious and to learn," said Jean- Louis Dubler. Grainne Dubler added: "The new facilities are also designed to encourage students to think about sustainable development – from the solar panels on the roof to the biotope which will help in the conservation of frogs. The 'Discovery Garden' funded by the parents' association for the growing of fruits and vegetables promotes healthy eating."

The Haut-Lac family has recently introduced another pioneering facility. It's a bilingual daycare nursery in Vevey from 18 months and which invites children to "explore, discover and grow" as they take their first steps into the adventure that is education.

There is a further family connection, Grainne Dubler and Anne-Marie Harwood are sisters who are originally from Northern Ireland. It is fitting that the concept of education at Haut- Lac is taken from a quote attributed to Irish poet W.B. Yeats (1865-1939) - "Education is not the filling of a pail but the lighting of a fire."

Institute Monte Rosa

57 avenue Chillon
CH-1820 Territet/Montreux
Tel 021 965 45 45
info@monterosa.ch
www.monterosa.ch

Bernhard Gademann who lives in Veytaux - a commune where Chillon Castle is located, is the third generation of educators. He is director of the eminent Monte Rosa, the independent school for boys and girls which was established in 1874.

Monte Rosa is an international boarding school for children from 9 to 19 years. It gained its excellent reputation because it offers individualised teaching for each child. Therefore the students can develop their own personality at their own pace, hone their social skills and learn to shoulder their share of responsibility in life. The small classes which consist of between two to 10 students promote motivation and encourage them to take pride and pleasure in their work. In all, the learning environment provides an academic programme suited to each student's needs.

"The students of today have access to all forms of information systems from iPads to laptops and mobile phones," he said. "We don't ban these things in the classroom. But we ask them to respect others in their use. Don't disrupt the class but be discrete. In spite of modern technology, all you need to educate is two chairs and a table. One chair for the teacher and another for the student."

HIM Hotel Institute Montreux

Avenue des Alpes 15
1820 Montreux
Phone +41 (0)21 966 46 46
Fax +41 (0)21 966 46 00
administration@him.ch
www.him.ch

HIM offers an internationally recognized Swiss Diploma in Hotel Operations Management and a Swiss Higher Diploma in Hospitality Management. Together with its partner Northwood University in Florida, a dual BBA degree in Business Administration and Hotel, Restaurant and Resort Management: a winning combination of Swiss style Hospitality and American Management training.

Swiss Hotel Management School S.H.M.S.

Caux-Palace Rue du Panorama 2
1824 Caux
Phone +41 (0)21 962 95 55
Fax +41 (0)21 962 95 56
info@shms.com
www.shms.com

SHMS is Switzerland's largest English-speaking Hotel Management School. It offers a wide range of world-class academic programmes for undergraduates and postgraduates in Hospitality, Events and Tourism Management. The Swiss and Higher Diploma combine theoretical and practical modules, including two internships for valuable industry experience.

The BA (hons) Degree in Hospitality, Tourism or Events Management and the Master's Degree in Hospitality Management are both awarded in collaboration with the University of Derby (UK).

European University

Grand-Rue 3
1820 Montreux
Phone +41 (0)21 964 84 64
Fax +41 (0)21 964 84 68
info@euruni.edu
www.euruni.edu

European University (EU) is one of the world's top business schools renowned for the excellence of its students and faculty. EU is a triple accredited, international business school with main campuses in Montreux, Geneva, Barcelona and Munich in addition to partnership programs around the globe. The university has been developing quality business education for over 40 years through its experienced faculty and pragmatic approach.

European University was established in 1973 in Antwerp by Xavier Nieberding and in 1982 in Brussels by Dean Dominique Jozeau. The current president and UNESCO Chair in International Relations, Business Administration and Entrepreneurship is Dr. Dirk Craen. After joining as an adjunct faculty member in 1977, Craen became professor and dean at the Montreux Campus in 1985 and new president in 1998. (See entry Dr Dirk Craen)

Prospective international students can

European University Business School

find management, business and finance programmes at the Business Foundation (BF), Bachelor's (BBA), Master's (MBA) and Doctoral (DBA) levels in Switzerland.

European University Montreux's curriculum promotes the managerial skills, business ethics and entrepreneurial initiative vital to finding jobs in the current and future global markets.

It combines the American university model with the top European management practices to offer students the necessary tools to be successful in the international business world.

European University Montreux's practical and hands-on educational programmes include management theory and case studies and are taught by international faculty members who are experts in the fields of Business Administration, Communication, Public Relations, Hospitality, Finance, Sports Management and International Relations.

Glion Institute of Higher Education

118 Rue du Lac
1815 Clarens
Tel 021 989 2677
info@glion.edu
www.glion.edu

Judy Hou is an outstanding example of the new generation of women who have risen to become top executives of major corporations. GM, IBM, Hewlett Packard and Pepsico are all headed by female CEOs. They comprise only some 8% worldwide.

Today, Glion-Institute of Higher Education which is part of the Laureate Universities, an education provider with 75 higher education institutions and a student population of over 800,000, is headed by Judy Hou. She is a high-powered CEO who has had extensive experience of over 20 years in hospitality and education. Her background is ideal as she has worked within a variety of departments at big brands such as Park Hyatt, Mandarin Oriental and Swiss hotels. On the education front, she has a BA degree in Liberal Arts from Columbia university, New York which counts President Barack Obama as an alumni; a masters degree in hospitality administration from Lausanne Hospitality School where she also worked as an assistant professor and researcher; and is currently completing her doctorate in Business Administration online at Walden university.

"In this borderless world, institutions like Glion provide endless career opportunities," said Judy Hou. "The semesters and the internship can be spent anywhere in the world. We have just opened a London campus and besides Montreux,we also have a Chicago campus. Apropos internships abroad, we have a department which sole purpose is to place students globally. Then with this combination of academic and real-world learning, graduates are ready to step straight into jobs and work immediately as professionals. Some 86% receive offers on the day they graduate including from top companies like Louis Vuitton, JP Morgan Chase and the World Economic Forum."

Glion was founded more than 50 years ago in1962 by Walter Hunziker and Frédéric Tissot who were Swiss tourism pioneers. They envisioned the need for professional hotel managers and set about building one of the finest hospitality management schools in the world. Today, it offers management-focused programmes for hospitality and other service industries.

"We transform the young students from young adults into young professionals," she said. "Glion, is European in outlook, Swiss in its work ethos, American in its educational approach and multinational in its student body. Nationalities comprise Europe 55%, Asia- Pacific 24%, Middle East and Africa 11% and the Americas 10%."

Hou, an American of Chinese descent speaks perfect Mandarin, English, and Spanish. She comes from an entrepreneurial family. Her father was a civil engineer who owns a construction and architecture company with her mother. If there was something that was taught in the family, it was initiative and resourcefulness.

In 2001, she was appointed CEO of the Les Roches Jin Jiang hotel management college, Shanghai, a joint venture between Les Roches and Jin Jiang International Hotels, China's leading hotel company. Hou's recent appointment in 2013 at Glion Institute of Higher Education may also herald a new era for hospitality and education in Switzerland.

Le Liboson

1824 Caux
Tel 021 963 3019
www.liboson.ch

Liboson is a cultural centre located in one of the most magnificent spots above Montreux. The centre is in the medieval chalet of Paul and Nicole du Marchie van Voorthuysen who are in a quest of beauty hand-in-hand with music, art and philosophy. Paul who came from a privileged background in The Netherlands, is much travelled - he spent time with nomads in the Sahara desert, the monks in Mount Athos and studied the civilization of ancient Egypt. He together with Nicole who is an author and an accomplished painter and musician provide different cultural courses as well as evening events.

The centre also offers accommodation in its large guest room with kitchen and bathroom. It is ideal place for a retreat with its library of 2,000 volumes and quiet surroundings. The ambiance with its mysterious corridors, Egyptian crypt and 70 doors enables guests to enter a timeless world.

Nicole and Paul du Marchie van Voorthuysen

1

Clinique La Prairie

Clinics

Clinique La Prairie

1815 Clarens-Montreux
021 989 3311
info@laprairie.com
www.laprairie.com

There are clinics and clinics but none can measure up to the most exclusive Clinique La Prairie. It's a fascinating world of its own between the shore of Lake Geneva and the snow-capped peaks of the Swiss Alps.

The four buildings which comprise the clinic include the modern glass high-tech medical centre, the 5-star Chateau hotel, the Residence which houses the laboratories and the Richter and Rocha Dahl terraced extension which connects them all. The main reception, spa cafe and restaurant are situated in the extension with its seductive cool interior decor, kidney-shaped blue pool and which is surrounded by a landscaped French garden.

The range of health and body care is extraordinary from plastic surgery, gynaecology, cardiology, dentistry, orthopaedics, thalassotherapy, psychiatry, acupuncture and reflexology to medical checkups and programmes for beauty, weight management and better mobility. But revitalisation - a four day treatment, which established its reputation of over the past eight decades is at the heart of its activities.

The programmes tend to be costly but what price can you put on good health and anti- ageing.

Rise in businessmen clients

Vincent Steinmann, the communication,

marketing and sales director, has a background in the Big Four accountancy firms such as PricewaterhouseCoopers and KPMG. The companies fostered high performance cultures with people who were globally minded.

"I have discovered interesting trends at Clinique La Prairie," he said. "More and more top businessmen with back-to-back meetings and tight travel schedules are turning to our DNA - revitalization," he said. "Last year, men clients almost equaled the women, 48% to 52%. What is even more to the point, these hard working executives take care of themselves. They are anticipatory of the problems and have a list of do's and don'ts. Prevention is better than cure is their credo."

One local resident and his wife have come regularly to the Health Club for the past 18 years. They never installed a swimming pool, sauna or hamam in their home because they prefer to use the facilities at Clinique La Prairie. The fitness coach provides a personal programme which is changed frequently so that all their muscle groups are exercised.

"I would suggest a week stay to experience our DNA which can keep people going for up to two years," he said. "In fact, I'm proud of our loyalty record. Some 60% return."

Revitalisation Man

Dr Adrian Heini is the medical director of Clinique La Prairie. He follows in the footsteps of Professor Paul Niehans who established the clinic over 80 years ago and was a pioneer in cellular therapy for the "rejuvenation" programme. But a lot has changed over the decades as patients' lives have speeded up and there is more stress and frustration.

Today, La Prairie Clinic is a one-stop clinic where high-tech meets holistic medicine. Where else can you have a Thai massage, seaweed treatment, botox, aqua-gym class, sleep consultation, yoga, a hip replacement in a relaxing atmosphere on the shore of Lake Geneva.

"Clinique La Prairie is a medical establishment which uses specific treatments to provide specific solutions," said Dr Adrian Heini. "We've continued the tradition of the holistic concept in medicine which takes into account all aspects of a person's needs including psychological, physical and social and they are seen as a whole."

Dr Heini studied medicine at the University hospital in Lausanne (CHUV) and specialised in internal medicine, specifically clinical nutrition at Cambridge university (where he measured metabolism of populations in Africa) and the University of Alabama, Birmingham, USA. He has worked at the Clinique La Prairie since 1999 and was appointed Medical Director in 2010.

"Montreux is a fantastic place for a clinic as it's not overcrowded," he said, "easy in terms of traffic and with a lot of international events and visitors. Above all, there are no extremes in climate. It's balanced, a microclimate which suits our luxury wellness concept with a relaxing spa. The views of snow-capped peaks of the Swiss Alps and Lake Geneva are part of the cure."

The clinic's various medical programmes consists of a variety of personalised treatments which teaches patients how best to look after their health, find the balance necessary for a harmonious life and to preserve their youth. For example, take the case of a woman in her thirties who suffers some stress, poor sleep and would not mind losing some kilos. Soon after arrival, she has an hour consultation with a dietician who explains that food is not just for nourishment, it tackles disease and ageing. She is encouraged to enjoy eating and not to count calories. But never to feel full or uncomfortable after a meal. Later, she has an interview with Dr Heini whose specialism is clinical nutrition, energy metabolism and obesity. She tells him she is burnt-out from a hectic travel schedule. He suggests yoga, light sport, massage and emphasises that she should follow the nutritionist's advice.

"The Latin maxim "Mens sana in corpore sano" - a healthy mind in a healthy body is still relevant today," said Dr Heini. "Physical activity is essential for a healthy life. It creates a sense of wellbeing and energy. Combine the mind with the body. The malaise appears when there is an imbalance either in the social and/or professional life. It's usually a sign of too much stress and the fact that people are unaware of the inherent frustrations. The mission at the clinic is not just weight loss but to modify lifestyle. Sometimes a patient who has a sweet tooth, suffers from sugar withdrawal and tells me that they feel guilty about their addiction to chocolates. I remind them that it's just psychological. In the same way, I think that a lot of so-called allergies such as wheat are in the head.

The Revitalisation programme is unique and has put the Clinique La Prairie clinic ahead of the competition. But it only can be applied from the age of 40 with results lasting from one to two years. It helps to increase youthfulness by revitalising the body in depth. For people under great stress or under intense workloads, it can be applied to those under 40. As a result, the programme appeals to top decision-makers as they can indulge in a treatment that boosts vitality, immune function and libido while banishing fatigue and the effects of ageing.

"For a change these executives can make the right decision for themselves," said Dr Heini. "More and more men are coming for revitalisation treatments. The attraction is to increase performance levels. We promote evidence-based medicine."

Dr Adrian Heini is a perfect example of the "revitalisation man." He is slim and enjoys exercise but has never been an athlete. He believes in moderation in all things, specially in food and alcohol. Above all, he has a balance in life - even the location with its microclimate is in equilibrium. He lives in Blonay with his wife, two daughters and a son. He is the right man with the right qualifications to head the prestigious medical spa with its holistic vision of health for a better quality of life

Laclinic Montreux

Avenue de Collonge 43
1820 Montreux-Territet
Tel 021 966 7000
info@placlinic.ch
www.laclinic.ch

Laclinic-Montreux is a beauty clinic where you will find all the medical treatments dedicated to beauty under one roof: plastic surgery, aesthetic dentistry and implantology, aesthetic medicine and dermatology, a laser centre and microsurgical hair transplantation. In addition, Laclinic provides stem cell treatments, medical check-ups and revitalisation cures.

"Art plays an important part in my work," said Dr Pfulg. "My yardstick is Leonardo Da Vinci who measured beauty by calculating perfect proportions. He unlocked the secret of divine beauty when he illustrated a book on proportions in nature. He divided the face into three equal parts. The first goes from the top of the forehead to the eyebrows, the second from eyebrows to the base of the nose and the third from the base of the nose to the bottom of the chin. Each of these parts should be of equal length.

"Symmetry is the key to beauty. Take the example of Kate Moss. What makes her so gorgeous? Is it her perfectly sculpted cheekbones? Retroussé nose or almond shaped eyes? Kate Moss is nearly perfect but her mouth should be 2 mm wider. Other seductive women who have ideal proportions include Elizabeth Hurley, Sienna Miller and Sonia Mbele, the

Generations star. Victoria Beckham is outside this category because her broad mid-face is disproportionate to the rest of her features."

An interesting feature of Laclinic-Montreux is that it recommends beauty treatments alongside aesthetic medicine and plastic surgery. Dr Pfulg considers complementary cosmetic treatments essential. Laclinic has developed PHI-cosmeceuticals - a day and night cream which looks after and preserves your skin. In 2008, Helena Rubinstein (L'Oreal Group) combined the excellence of its own laboratories with the know-how and talent of Dr. Pfulg. This unprecedented scientific partnership in anti-aging expertise gave rise to Re-Plasty. It's a range of Helena Rubinstein with anti-aging cosmetic innovations that complements the aesthetic medicine.

Biotonus Clinique

Bon Port 27 Montreux
Tel 021 966 5858
www.biotonus.ch

Biotonus is a private clinic situated in the quiet surroundings of the Hôtel Du Grand Lac Excelsior on the shores of lake Geneva. Dr Reza Tavassoli began his collaboration in 1984. It's a leading Swiss clinic that offers anti-ageing treatments, detox and weight loss programs as well as treatments for stress, depression and addiction.

The unique combination of a hotel and a private clinic is well suited to the holistic approach to patient cares. There are 87 spacious rooms including suites and junior suites with modern facilities and offer splendid views on the lake and the Alps. The wellness section includes a half-size Olympic indoor swimming pool which is heated to 28°C, a sauna, a steam room and a wellness centre.

The medical team consists of six doctors and some 20 nurses, dieticians, radiological technicians, a physiotherapist, among others.

"Before each treatment, patients go through a thorough medical check-up," said Dr Tavassoli." The result of the tests give us a good idea of the patient's health status and we can proceed with the appropriate treatment. In addition, they also receive a daily program of some 15 therapies which includes aqua gymnastics, sophrology, yoga, body detox, massages etc. to ascertain which they prefer. We then can personalise the programme."

During their stay, the patients have the benefit of psychological support, targeted nutritional training, relaxation sessions and body care that includes regular physical activity. A special diet is planned according to the patient's needs.
"There is a saying that you dig your own grave with your teeth," said Dr Tavassoli. "Obesity costs a lot to society as it can cause diabetes and cardiovascular disease, among other problems. At Biotonus, our treatments can stabilise a patient's weight, balance their metabolism with guidance towards a healthy life style."

Nurse station Biotonus Clinique

Christmas Market

Events

Montreux Jazz Festival

Avenue Claude Nobs 3-5
1820 Montreux
Tel 021 966 4444
www.montreuxjazzfestival.com

The event is one of the biggest and most famous in the world, featuring world-class artists from B.B.King to Stevie Wonder and takes place over two weeks in early July. Over its four decades it has retained its jazz label while branching out to include rock, soul, funk and blues musicians.

There is a combination of paying venues such as the auditorium Stravinsky which is humongous space and the free stages, clubbing and workshops which spring up on the lakefront. There are two new platforms, the Montreux Jazz club and the Montreux Jazz lab. The first is a touchstone of the festival which showcases major talents, songwriters as well as the next generation of jazzers. The second is interactive and in-your-face with a mix of audiovisual experiments, edgy concerts and incredible artists.

Montreux is turned upside down during the festival with huge car parks set up on the outskirts served by free buses. Special train and bus services are run every night for visitors from other parts of Switzerland.

The entry should be read in conjunction with other texts in People section on Mathieu Jaton, Thierry Amsallem, Michel Ferla, François Michel, Laurent Wehrli, among others and the Montreux Jazz Cafe and the Bazar Suisse where souvenirs can be bought.

Queen who recorded a total of seven albums at Mountain studios is now located in the Casino Barrière Monttreux. The control room has been re-created and is part of an exhibition which includes the original sound equipment as well as photos and memorabilia.

1

Montreux Noël Christmas Market

Grand Rue 24
CH 1820
Tel 021965 2412
info@montreuxnoel.com
www.montreuxnoel.com

Father Christmas in Lapland, Finland now has a rival in Switzerland. The Christmas market in Montreux from the end of November to December 24 offers similar entertainment for children and families. They can meet Father Christmas in his house and be given a present with a certificate and promise to be good over the next year. There are two advantages over Lapland, less travel time and a milder climate. Instead of two flights of over four hours from the UK, it's only one flight of 1.5 hours and a short train journey. The venue of Montreux Noel is in the microclimate of Montreux instead of the harsh winter temperatures which can drop to -20 or -40. Montreux Noel also provides a magical, festive atmosphere with snow-based activities. In addition, families have the added attraction of fascinating medieval entertainment at Chillon Castle and less travel time.

They can take the special train up to visit Father Christmas in Rochers-de-Naye at 2,032 m. There they can experience an unforgettable moment like face painting, a photo with Father Christmas, a certificate and hunt for treasure. In the Christmas village at Caux, they are welcomed by a real Lap dressed in costume and his reindeer. They can participate in the Christmas workshop and make candles and other things. Admire a giant nativity scene and walk in an enchanted forest. While they are there they have an opportunity to watch shows including Snick the clown. On the lake shore there are 150 chalets, each with regional specialities and artisans, music, wine tasting and loads of presents to select. A fascinating trip can be taken to Chillon Castle where they can experience the medieval atmosphere as people are dressed in costumes including knights in armour, jugglers, jesters and other entertainers.

The market abounds with all sorts of restaurants and there is no shortage of cuisines. The food includes meats cooked on a spit, raclette and fondue, surf and turf, game, wines including mulled wine as well as the usual pizzas and hamburgers. In all, the Montreux Christmas market is a fabulous treat for both parents and specially children who will be open-mouthed at the spectacular event.

September Classical Musical

The Montreux-Vevey music festival September musical which was founded in 1946, takes place end of August and beginning of September. The Director is Prof. Tobias Richter.

Information

+41 (0)21 962 80 00
info@septmus.ch

Box Office

+41 (0)21 962 80 05
Monday to Saturday
from 10am to 3pm (May - October)
Email: billetterie@septmus.ch

Montreux Comedy

Tel 021964 5972
info@montreuxcomedy.ch
www.montreuxcomedy.ch

Charlie Chaplin in Ulan Bator

Comedy festival in Montreux? You must be joking. Yes, its bigger on the web than the Montreux Jazz Festival and the Cannes Film Festival. Who's behind it? A brilliant chap called Grégoire Furrer.

Comedy is the rock 'n' roll of the Y generation. Every young person on the planet is on YouTube filming their material. It doesn't matter where they live or what language they speak but they all do some of their stuff in English. They know that's how they'll get worldwide attention. In the forefront of this is Grégoire Furrer's Montreux Comedy Festival. The lineup this year, has the big stars of African comedy in the programme Stand Up Africa: Loyiso Gola, Kagiso Lediga, Stuart Taylor, David Kibuuka and Joseph Opio.

The Montreux Comedy Festival also has a contest to find new talent. This includes an Awards ceremony in which the winner is chosen by a jury and the audience which sees the performance on YouTube and on the stage. During the four days of the festival, two venues are used including the Montreux Music and Convention Centre and the Théâtre de Poche de la Grenette, Vevey.

Montreux Music and Convention Centre

Avenue Claude Nobs 5
Tel 021 962 2000
www.2m2c.ch

Montreux has a good reputation as an international convention, music and cultural centre. The lakeside town's facilities are superb for high-profile gatherings like the summit of the Francophone nations, the Syrian peace talks,the bilateral trade agreements between Switzerland and China, the Middle East nations talks on denuclearisation of the region and secret talks between the Russian Parliament and Chechen officials. It features music events like the famous Montreux Jazz festival, the Classical concerts, the choral festival and cultural events such as the Comedy festival.

The Montreux Music and Convention Centre (2m2c) is a prime and ideal venue for all events. It's an exceptional site of 18,000 square metres and consists of two buildings. The Miles Davis hall is suitable for 100 to 500 people and the Stravinsky auditorium which can accommodate 300 to 3,000 people and has a reputation for its perfect acoustics. Besides, the convention spaces, it had two exhibition halls, with a combined area of 4,000 square metres, dressing rooms for performers and parking for organisers. The big advantage is that the 2m2c centre is within walking distance of hotels, restaurants, the station, the Casino and the lake promenade. It's also in a stunning location with amazing views of the lake and Alps from its large terraces.

Montreux is also well placed for excursions as within an hour radius you are in what is considered to be a miniature Switzerland. Visitors can enjoy the essential elements of Swissness - chocolates, cheese and watchmaking. Within 20 minutes, they can see a cheese factory in Gruyere and the Cailler-Nestlé chocolate factory. Within 40 minutes they can be in the watchmaking area of Yverdon les Bains.

"Our strength is the brand Montreux which is known worldwide, thanks to Claude Nobs and the Montreux Jazz Festival," said Rémy Crégut, the General Manager of Montreux Music and Convention Centre (2m2c). "Our setting is unique. You take the train from the plane in Geneva and everything else is within walking distance. There's free bus rides if you have luggage or prefer transport. Our weakness is that the destination is not known. As a small town and may not have the biggest choice of restaurants, shops and other entertainments. But Lausanne is half hour away and offers it."

Rémy Crégut who comes from the Camargue, France is a high flyer in sales and marketing. He has wealth of experience not only in the hotel industry but also in conference centres. He was sales director of the largest Accor hotel, the 650 bedroomed Sofitel Porte de Sevres in 1989. The next three years, he was with Hyatt Regency as director of sales and marketing, first in Casablanca and then in Paris CDG, Roissy Airport where he was responsible for setting up the pre-opening strategy. In 1993, he was back in Paris at the Grand Hotel Intercontinental and accountable for a budget of $50 million. The hotel had 550 rooms and three restaurants including the famous Cafe de la Paix and the oldest banqueting room in the city. He was commended on his performance as the hotel became the most profitable in the Intercontinental chain.

One of the biggest challenges of his career was the position with Disneyland Paris Business Solutions. Over three years, he established the new business unit dedicated to corporate events in seven hotels, 44 restaurants, the convention centre, the golf course and the theme park. In addition, he opened a new convention centre. The turnover almost doubled in his tenure of office to $45 million from $25 million. From 1999 to 2005, he held various positions including the Grimaldi Forum in Monaco before he joined Montreux Music and Conventions Centre in 2006.

"When we hosted the Syrian peace talks," he said, "we were expecting 300 journalists at the press centre in 2m2c. Over a 1,000 turned up! That's my job to imagine what's not imaginable. Consequently, there was a 2% increase in internet usage in Switzerland. One of the biggest events is the Montreux Jazz Festival which attracts over 100,000 visitors over 15 days. What I like about it, is the informality of the musicians facilitated by the unique atmosphere. You can meet them and have a chat. That's how I ended up talking with the pop star, Paulo Nutini, at Harry's bar."

Rémy Crégut is the right man, at the right place, at the right time. If anyone can make a big success of 2m2c, he can. He is a leading sales and marketing director with international expe rience. He is proud that he realised some of his dreams as a young man. One of them was to participate in the Paris to Dakar race which he achieved on a Yamaha in 1982. His business philosophy? "You're dead if you don't rethink yourself and your business on a daily basis."

Excursions

Goldenpass

rue de la gare 22
Montreux
Tel 0219898181
www.goldenpass.ch

Goldenpass is a big plus to any visit to the Montreux Riviera. The rail company offers funicular services, rack-and pinion rides and a choice of classic 19th century and ultra- modern panoramic trains. But the highlight of any trip surely is the 'Chocolate Train' which enables the tourist to see the essentials of Swissness. It offers a visit to a chocolate and cheese factory. The only thing missing is a visit to valley de Joux which can be compensated by joining a watchmaking class at Lionel Meylan, Vevey.

"We're a narrow gauge railway company and don't require wide tunnels through the mountains," said Grégoire Clivaz, PR. "We were established over a century ago when the British were the first tourists and stayed in the grand hotels in Caux, Glion and Mont Pèlerin. Nowadays, its the Chinese and Indian tourists who are in the forefront. Each culture has its own needs.

The Chinese, for example, prefer to eat their own cuisine and require hot water on our trains for their packet soups."
There are two short excursions by Goldenpass. A 55-minute journey on a cog railway will take you from Montreux up to Rochers-de-Naye (2,042 m.), a rocky balcony that offers spectacular views of Lake Geneva, the Alps and the Jura. On top, there are a variety of activities including biking, hiking, skiing, climbing on the Via Ferrata and visiting the Alpine garden, marmots in the park, the Christmas market, father Christmas or dining in the panoramic restaurant which has accommodation including Mongolian yurts. (Tel 021 989 8190)

Another excursion from Vevey will take you to Les Pléiades (1,348 m.) where the theme is the stars. From the window of the train you can see unique views of Lake Geneva, fields of narcissi or snowscapes. The restaurant offers a good selection of meals as well as homemade tarts. It is managed by François Relet and provides accommodation. (Tel 021 926 8070) It's a departure point for hikes and the constellation discovery trail that will teach you about astronomy. Winter is an exceptional time because it becomes a wonderland for skiing, snowboarding, sledging, snow shoeing, cross country skiing, hiking or walking. Visitors can return by foot to Blonay.

The chocolate train which runs from May to October includes the famous Gruyère cheese factory and Cailler, Broc - one of the oldest chocolate factories. There is also a chance to see Gruyère, a beautiful medieval town. The day excursion lasts from 8.57 am to 5.33 pm. and visitors return stimulated by the different flavours of cheese and chocolate.

"The newest service is the cheese train (Montreux/Chateau - d'Oex)," said Doriane Kohli, Marketing Manager, "that offers visitors an opportunity to see and taste the much-loved Alpine Etivaz which

GOLDENPASSLINE

Classic train

is still made over an open wood fire. The inclusive package from December to April starts with a glass of wine and cheese at the departure of 10.14. The cheese making is followed by an organic fondue lunch and a visit to the private museum where visitors can experience the ambiance of traditional homes and admire the handmade cut-outs. (Decoupage à la main.)"
The three funicular routes cover one of the oldest, the Territet-Glion line, which was established in 1883. In Glion it is recommend to visit the magnificent Victoria hotel where visitors will find a true Belle Epoque establishment. The other two funiculars pass through the Unesco Lavaux vineyards including the vintner's village of Chardonne and Les Avants-Sonloup where passengers can enjoy one of the most picturesque hiking regions .

The company also has long distance excursions to Gstaad and Lucerne.

"Goldenpass is a private company which provides public transport and develops tourism," said George Oberson, director. "We carry over five million passengers a year and are successful because of the dedication and innovation of our staff."

Wine Tours

Swiss Riviera Wine Tours

Avenue des Alpes 43
1820 Montreux
Tel 021 965 32 37
info@swissrivierawinetours.com

The Lavaux wine region with its spectacular vineyard terraces is listed by UNESCO as part of the World Heritage. Swiss Riviera Wine Tours organises fun and educational private wine tours at historical wine domaines and chateaus and include wine tastings and generous vineyard picnics.

There are three options. The Join-in Wine tour which is held only on Monday with a minimum of four participants and costs CHF 225 a person. The Private Wine Tour from two to 12 people with degressive pricing. This can consist of a half day chateau and wine tour or the Lavaux (UNESCO) vineyard tour or a whole day with an exclusive winemaker's lunch. The third option is a group or corporate event from five to 500 people.

"We specialise in customised tours for guests seeking a unique Swiss experience accompanied by a great guide," said Nicolas Abundo, who is the Director of Swiss Riviera Wine Tours. "The Chablais and Lavaux vineyards are picturesque and views from some of the high vineyards are stunning. We also have keys to Aigle castle, private tastings at Chateau Chillon and various private wine estates which gives us access at any time and allow us to present the best of Switzerland. Another aspect of the Lavaux vineyards is the fact that it's the first vineyard to receive a UNESCO certification as well as being a 'Google World of Wonder.'"

Swiss wines are relatively unknown because little of it's small production is exported. If you want to learn about the wines, know about the cultural and historical aspects of the region and indulge

1

in a good 'terroir aperitif' of Swiss specialities (including the famous Swiss chocolate) with red wine after your walk, then a private wine tour is recommended.

Oron Castle

Au château 1
1608 Oron-le-Châtel
Tel 021 907 9051
www.swisscastles.ch/Vaud/Oron

Open April - September, Saturday and Sunday. Visits for groups can be arranged at other times. Functions can be held in the four rooms on the ground floor.

The 12th century Oron castle is well worth a visit because of its authentic ambiance and fascinating objects d'art. The top floor which has a set of historic rooms is filled with furniture and paintings including the hunting room with its 19th century wallpaper depicting hunting scenes; the music room with a harp and a Pleyel piano from the 18th century which belonged to Frederic Chopin; the bedroom of Alice Paquelier Gaiffe with a baldaquin over the bed and famous miniatures and watercolours on its walls; and the kitchen with a fireplace large enough to roast an ox together with rotary serving hatches.

The pièce de résistance is the magnificent library of 18,000 volumes complete with first editions of novels published between 1780-1825. A prized collection is the complete set of Diderot encyclopaedia which are illustrated with great detail e.g. how the Gobelin tapestry factory worked. (The catalogue is online: http://dbserv1-bcu.unil.ch/oron/oron.php)

The castle was also the home of a latter-day Jeanne d'Arc, Catherine von Wattenwyl (1645-1714) who was born into an old aristocratic Bernese family. As a girl, she was more interested in guns than in dolls and grew up to be a sharp shooter, a duelist and a horsewoman. She was a great admirer of King Louis XIV and undertook secret missions for him. Accused of being spy, she was imprisoned, tortured and sentenced to death. However, her family intervened and she was exiled to Valangin castle, Neuchatel, where she lived for 22 years. There she wrote her memoirs which was completed four days before she died. She was wed twice but her family prevented her from marrying her great love, Charles von Diesbach who was a catholic and captain of the Swiss guard.

In 1870, Adolphe Gaiffe (1830-1903), a Frenchman, bought the castle as a summer home. A bibliophile and a friend of Victor Hugo, he built the library to house his collection of books. An important part which comprised a third of the total belonged to a Polish princess, Helena Apolonia Potocka (1763-1815). She was the niece of the Archbishop of Vilnius and educated in Paris at l'Abbaye du Bois.

The castle was bought in 1934 by the Association pour la Conservation du château d'Oron, which was founded to preserve the castle and has some 1,000 members. The chairman is André Locher and the association should be congratulated for the wonderful work it has done with conservation over eight decades.

Library Oron Castle ©www.Swisscastles.ch

Catherine von Wattenwyl ©www.Swisscastles.ch

Glacier 3000

Col du Pillon
CH-1865 Les Diablerets
Tel 024 492 3377
info line 0848 00 3000
Info@glacier3000.ch
www.glacier3000.ch

The glacier 3000 is an unmissable sight for tourists who come to the Montreux Riviera. It perfectly compliments the glory of the lakeside as it offers the Alpine spectacle of seeing 24 top peaks including the famous Matterhorn, the highest mountain in Europe - Mont Blanc as well as triple summits of the Eiger, Mönch and Jungfrau.

"The spectacular view can be seen from the world's first suspension bridge, Peak Walk, to connect two mountain peaks," said Claudia von Siebenthal, marketing and sales manager." It connects Glacier 3000 with Scex Rouge at 9,800 ft above sea level. The bridge is designed to survive extreme weather conditions such as heavy snow and high winds."

Glacier 3000 is a dual season attraction which is open year-round. You can ski from end of October to the beginning of May with 10 installations and 30 km of ski runs. It is a paradise for freeriders and cross country skiers who can enjoy perfect conditions on the Tsanfleuron glacier. Other activities include a dog sled ride, the snow bus and the adrenalin-throbbing bobsleigh ride with the Alpine coaster. In addition, there is a watch and souvenir shop and a restaurant. It can be reached in about 40 minutes from Montreux by car.

Lavaux vineyards ©Pierre Bise

TIVAL DES ARTISTES DE RUE
22-23-24 AOÛT
RUE PIETONN
REDKEN
LANDLER

Chapter 2. Vevey

History

"Vevey ..... is paradise and I don't see how people there and at Lausanne can have the impudence to suppose that they go to heaven after death." Edward Lear, artist and author who passed through the town on his way to Rome in 1837**.**

Vevey occupies a beautiful location at the mouth of the Veveyse valley and at the foot of the Mt Pélerin. Its centre is the market square, Place du Marché, which was the site of the old grain market, the Grenette (1808) and where local traders hold a market twice a week - Tuesdays and Saturdays. The town has the distinction having an unrestricted view onto the lake. A city ordinance bans any building from

Charlie Chaplin statue and Laurent Ballif, Mayor of Vevey

being higher than the ground on which the church of St Martin stands.

Old Town Vevey

Vevey is the capital of the famous Lavaux wine growing region and once a generation (roughly every 20 years), the Place du Marché vibrates with excitement. It's the Brotherhood of Winegrowers festival which dates back to the 18th century, an event over 2 /3 weeks and involves thousands of actors and dancers. The next is scheduled for 2019.

Vevey is an old-fashioned town unlike its posh neighbour Montreux and the old town east of the square is worth a visit. Many of the shops remind one of Paris in the 1960s. Writers have been inspired by the place from Nikolai Gogol (Dead Souls), W.M.Thackeray (The Newcomes), Dostoevsky (The Gambler), Henry James (Daisy Miller) to Arnold Bennett (The Card) and Graham Greene who spent his last years there.

Henri Nestlé and Charlie Chaplin

Two important figures who have made an impact on the area are Henri Nestlé who founded the giant food company that bears his name and Charlie Chaplin who settled with his family and now will be commemorated by a museum.

Tschumi's masterpiece

"In a sense, our building is an expression of the company. It is the motor that drives our global business; it is the power-base for developing future business and brand strategy; it is the centre for financial and human resource management; it is the launch-pad for Research and Development...Built in Vevey, the birthplace of our business, it is a symbol of our heritage but also a powerful symbol of our ambitious future." Peter Brabeck-Letmathe, Nestlé Chairman

Great architecture stands the test of time and the Y-shaped Nestlé HQ (1960) is a fine example of Jean Tschumi's timeless elegance. One marvels at the lake-transparency of the reception area made possible by the massive strength of the girders and the magnificent views from the halls inside. Further, one is gobsmacked by the double spiral central staircase on the ground floor that rises through six floors and is capped by an eye of light at the top.

Nestlé HQ building ©Nestec S.A., Vevey

Tschumi's other innovation is the cooling system which uses water between 7-9º C from the lake. It is pumped from a depth of 90 m and circulates in the ceilings of the building. The structure was declared a national monument in 1980.

Richter & Dahl Rocha were responsible for the renovation of the Tschumi building in 2000 and their pièce de résistance, the liaison space, connected each floor of Tschumi's curvaceous building with those of the simple bar building added in 1977. Given the unequal ceiling heights of the two buildings, ramps fan out floor to floor to mediate the gaps, offering an amazing vista. There is a third building, a rotunda with a spiral staircase which houses the 550-seat restaurant that serves 1,400 meals a day. The lower part also serves as a health and wellbeing centre.

The Nestlé HQ was the second of Tschumi's office buildings (for which he won the Reynolds prize) after La Mutuelle Vaudoise (1956) in Lausanne. It was followed by EPFL auditorium (1962) and posthumously the World Health Organisation(1966) in Geneva with Pierre Bonnard. In 1962, at the age of 57, he died of a heart attack on the night train from Paris to Lausanne.

People
The Mayor

I died on June 30, 1973

Laurent Ballif who is the mayor of Vevey is proud of his ancestry. He can trace his descendants back to the 14th century and to a certain Jaquet da Cuaz who was working for the Bailli or mayor in Villeneuve, Fribourg. That is how the family name of Ballif was acquired. Now there is a complete circle because Laurent Ballif too is a mayor.

"More recently our family had two branches," he said, "an ecclesiastical which courted controversy and an academic. One member was a professor at the university of Lausanne who couldn't accept the introduction of politics into sermons and became a Mormon. He later immigrated to Utah in the US.

"My branch was from the academics and comprised notaries, professors of education and teachers. I was born in Lucens. But I didn't want to become a teacher and instead studied political science in Lausanne. I became a journalist and lived in different places in the canton before I came to Vevey in my 20s. In 1985, I became a member of the commune council and general secretary of the Socialist Party of Vaud in 1988."

Besides politics, Laurent's other passion was swimming and he taught himself to swim in the unheated Montétan swimming pool in Lausanne. He won his first competition at Bellerive when the swimming club of Léman Lausanne organised a competition to recruit new members. He has been hooked ever since on swimming competitions and became a professional coach.

At one time, he worked flat out on his two passions. From 8 am to 4 pm, he was in the office of the Socialist party. Then from 4 pm to 8 pm he was at the pool and sometimes worked until 11 pm as a politician. His wife Catherine put a stop to his over-the-top busyness by warning that he would not have time to see their children grow up. But he kept the role of technical director of Vevey Swimming, took a course in sports management and launched a project in 1995 for the Sydney Olympics in 2000. His team qualified for the Olympics and over the years established 25 Swiss records and won 50 national titles. During this period, their fundraising activities was stimulated by their success and by the time he left in 2002, they had raised CHF 150,000. Now the fundraising is running at CHF 400,000 - CHF 600,000.

"I have always used analogies of swimming in my work," he said. "Essentially, it has to do with longterm planning. A swimmer at the age of 10 knows that practice for competitions isn't a last-minute affair and that he has to plan a long time ahead. This method impacts on his homework and later in life. Another aspect about swimming is that it's about floating. Every movement in one direction creates a counter movement in another direction. With the breast stroke you float on a bubble and use water as a tool."

As a socialist politician, he refers to himself as an up-to-date old fashioned Marxist and uses the theory as a tool. He is a good choice for mayor as the city's population is mixed between the rich and affluent and the poor and unemployed. He has a policy of harmony as he doesn't want to create segregation in the city. There is an active cultural life of concerts, theatre performances and art exhibitions.

"I have encouraged alternative culture groups in the city," he said, " In fact, the artists are flourishing in the Vevey. I don't want to have ghettos. For example, we have a group called the RATS who are musicians and into the plastic arts - 'plasticians' and we allow them to use empty buildings for their events. Most events are supported by the city and are usually free of charge."

The population of Vevey comprises 43% foreign nationals with 137 nationalities. There were successive periods of immigration during which Italians, Spaniards, Portuguese, Tamils and people from the Balkans came to the city.

"People in Vevey are gentle and accepting of others," he said, "and foreign nationals are given a good welcome. It's the same with tourism and we have a multitude of attractions: The old city's unmissable - a choice of six museums, 14 art galleries and five cinemas and of course, the big events such as the Images festival, the Wine cultural festival about every 20 years and the markets which are held twice a week in the Place du Marché."

The name Vevey is derived from the Latin, bis via, because it is located at a fork of two roads. One going west to Burgundy in France and the other north to Basel and Germany. It became industrialised in the 19th century with the establishment of the Atelier de Constructions Mécaniques de Vevey which manufactured turbines, tractors and locomotives. The company began with a production of tins for the food giant Nestlé.

Vevey market

Laurent Ballif is an avid collector of diverse objects - a sort of magpie collection. However, the hobby stems from the fact that he is a passionate historian with varied interests. His collecting began with folk music and learning to play a banjo. Consequently, he has a collection of 78s of old music hall songs, over 5,000 European comics, books and postcards on the history of Vevey, among other things.

"I died on June 30, 1973, and all my life since then is a bonus," he said. "It was strange because it was a year of deaths for our family. Three months before I had my accident, my father died at 52 and my sister had a miscarriage. Then I dived from a seven-metre high board into the lake. The water wasn't deep enough and I broke my neck. In such cases, there are only 10% survivors and of those, only a few do not have serious consequences. I was fortunate and every day is a gift."

Monks of St Maurice

If there is someone among the people of the Swiss Riviera who can be called a patrician then that person is without doubt, François Margot. He has all the right credentials. His education, bearing, mode

François Margot

of dress and cultural tastes all point in that direction. He comes from a landowning family and lives in an old mansion of his ancestors along the quai de la Veveyse surrounded by their portraits and 19th furniture. He went to school at the Abbey St Maurice in the Valais, a bastion of classical education where he studied Latin literature and philosophy as well as French literature. Tacitus, Horace and Pliny easily trip off his tongue and the same can be said of Tocqueville, Constant and Madame de Stael.

"The monks of St Maurice's Abbey opened my mind," he said. "Now there are many windows. To be cultivated as much as possible is a commendable aim for it makes you conscious about how little you know in life. It also encourages you to go on and learn a little bit more each day."

François Margot studied law and has a busy practice in Vevey. He has co-founded 10 companies of which he is chairman of the board, mostly in the cultural area such as Association of the Lavaux World Hertitage Grandvaux, Foundation of the September Music Festival Montreux-Vevey, Foundation of Fine Arts Vevey, Foundation of the Brotherhood of Winemakers, the Conservatory of Lausanne, among others.

"I'm a liberal by persuasion," he said, " A real liberal who's able to think with complete liberty. You also need to be practical and have contact with reality. To have a foot on the ground."

But he admits to a passion in life. He is interested in music which is a way of living with something that is not intellectual. His tastes are varied from Baroque and chamber music to Hindemith, Boulez, Stockhausen or John Adams.

"It's important to develop the right side of the brain which is the intuitive, subjective and creative," he said. "That's where music comes in. A daily dose of music is worth more that an apple a day. The right side is intellectual, objective and analytical. But it's important to have a balance."

He is a stalwart of the Montreux Riviera community with its tradition, culture and tourism. His family is part of the Brotherhood of Winegrowers that dates from 1647. He is president of the 2019 Festival of the Winegrowers and both his grandfather and father have also been involved on the board and in the former festivals. His musical activities included the eminent September Festival and he vowed that music for the 2019 Festival will be very present and consist of several composers.

However, he also has a crucial role in the economic welfare of the region through his presidency of the Montreux-Vevey Tourism. In this position, he provides leadership and direction to the team under Christoph Sturny.

"A tourist destination like Montreux-Vevey-Lavaux which has a lot of trump cards," he said, "doesn't build its reputation on one product. It constantly has to make a hierarchy in its strategy, define it's priorities and chose a lever of action. Your business life doesn't stand still. You don't undertake expeditions in unknown countries without a compass. Even having walked in touristic continents for decades, Montreux-Vevey Tourism still needs beacons."

Another "Leonardo da Vinci"?

Olivier Ferrari is a remarkable and imposing figure by any standards. He is a towering six and half footer with a matching ambition. His achievements are in the specialist field of pension funds, wealth management and sustainable development and is one of the top experts in Switzerland. In his lectures, he always gains immediate attention. His first slide is of planet earth taken from outer space. His maxim implants the image in the audience's mind, "Think global, act local and impact global." In another age, he would have been a good subject for a full length portrait like the Ambassadors by Hans Holbein.

Olivier Ferrari who lives in Vevey is the CEO of CONINCO, Explorers in finance SA. He is a financier with a difference and a great admirer of Leonardo de Vinci. In a way, he likes to emulate the artist. He too has several strings to his bow. The four sides of Olivier's business card says it all: Finance, Environment, Art and Philanthropy.

"When I was 9 years old I was impressed with Michelangelo and read all the books on his contemporary, Leonardo da Vinci," he said. "He was a polymath and a painter, sculptor, inventor, writer, engineer, anatomist, among other things. If I had another life, I would like to come back as Leonardo."

Olivier grew up in upper Vevey, Fully with his family. It was an Swiss Italian family and close as five fingers on the hand. He had a challenging career from the start. After studying science in Canton Fribourg, he was offered a job in a small bank. He had no title or job specification and was engaged only with the words, "We will see." They put him in charge of the real estate. As he progressed well, he was asked whether he would consider learning about pension asset management. The bank's choice was either to appoint a 40 year old with experience or Olivier (20) who would have to learn the business. He agreed and was sent to Basel for a year to study pension funds and pension investments.

"On the day I returned, I was ushered into an office by the director and handed a file," he said. "Here's a pension fund client and deal with him. I think on my feet and as I scanned the details, I began my spiel and bingo, I convinced my first client. I became one of the pioneers in the field with the development of an institutional asset management offering while I acted as an internal auditor of the bank's pension fund. Later, other opportunities opened up. I taught portfolio analysis on behalf of the Union of Regional Banks and created a structure to make pension funds more independent of their managers and to have greater control over their investment portfolio."

The Swiss pension system rests on three pillars. The first is the Old Age and Survivors' / Invalidity insurance while the second is the occupational pension scheme and the third is the private pension investment options. All three require mandatory contributions and the regulatory powers are limiting. Initially designed to be a minimum framework, the Swiss federal law on the pillars became more and more restrictive, thereby significantly limiting pension funds freedom of decision-making and increasing their costs. It appears to be restrictive but in reality, it is open and a wide range of opportunities are can be explored.

"You couldn't invest more than 50% in equities and 30% in foreign currency," he said, "an approach which was completely obsolete in the current global marketplace. Of course, you could exceed these limits if it was considered to be an exceptional case. But by the 1990s, the pension funds had become increasingly sophisticated on the investment side. This was due to the influence of the independent financial advisor like CONINCO."

He likes engaging in different issues and sustainable development was one of them. As a boy, he grew up in a forested area and at an early age gained a respect for nature.

"If I'm asked who my mentor is, I would answer a forest," he said. "A rainforest in fact. There, all the trees and plants are in equilibrium. They all have a place and none will beat the other. This concept inspired me in 1999, 2010 and 2011 to establish investment funds and opportunities which all focus on sustainable development. In 2007, I co-founded One Nature Foundation of which I'm Chairman of the Board. It provides an axis for a relationship between the economy and the environment based on forests, water and air. We can't fight the evolution of the economy so we have to integrate the factor of the environment in it."

His first picture moment occurred when he was 21 and saw a painting of horses by Hans Erni in a gallery. When he enquired the price, he found to his surprise that the cost was equivalent to a month's salary. Eventually after passing the gallery for months, he decided to buy the painting. A year later, he bought several paintings by the Israeli artist, Nissan Engel.

"I became a gallery owner by default," he said. "A friend wanted to organise an exhibition of his works at the Hotel des Berques in Geneva. I told him he could do something better and offered him my old office at Quai Perdonnet in Vevey. That's how the FERRARI ART GALLERY was established. It specialises in contemporary artists such as Ricardo Cordero, André Raboud, Franck Bouroullec, among others. My favourite modern sculptors are Henry Moore and Giacometti."

Olivier's main arena of innovation is as a financial specialist. In 1990, he founded CONINCO which is an advisory firm for institutional investors, asset valuation and responsible finance. The next step was to introduce socially responsible investment (SRI), corporate social responsibility

(CSR), and environmental and social governance criteria (ESG). The approach was intended to bring performances clients expect in line with new environmental, social and economic stakes.

"The establishment of ONE CREATION cooperative in 2010 was one of the most significant developments for sustainable and responsible growth," he said. "It was an opportunity to invest in companies to support economic activities while generating repeated and increasing revenues. It focused on longterm holdings in sectors such as renewable energies, waste and natural resources' management, new ecological materials etc. To cap all our efforts in this field, CONINCO became a signatory of the Principles for Responsible Investment (PRI) in 2014 which is supported by the United Nations." Then Olivier smiled and added," I wouldn't have been able to do all this without the support of my wife Sylvie and my two daughters."

Veveyian Soul

Anne-Christine Meylan runs L'Hostellerie de Geneve which is an institution in Vevey and is unmissable - 'à ne pas manquer.' It's a cafe, a bar, a restaurant, a hotel and is the epitome of the Veveyian soul. She is the only woman to own a hotel in Vevey.

"I'm lucky to be able to realise my dream of having my own place," said Anne-Christine Meylan who is a slip of a woman with a delightful vibrancy, "and to be able to express myself in this multi-layered hospitality."

Anne-Christine Meylan was born in Neuchatel and grew up in Morges. She studied at the Lausanne Hospitality School and her first positions were at top hotels in Crans-Montana: the Grand hotel Golf & Palace, at the opening of the Lindner Rhodania hotel and spa and the Crans Ambassador. After several years in the mountains, she longed to return to lake Geneva.

"I missed the lake and in 1984 after a search, I rented L'Hostellerie de Geneve," she said. "It had 11 bedrooms with separate toilets and was half the size it's now because the corner part was a grain shop with apartments above. I was able to expand into the grain shop in 1992 and after several years we were able to buy the whole building."

Each of the 23 bedrooms are unique and have a special theme. But fun is involved because the theme usually represents an adventure with Lionel. For example, the Venetian room resulted from a trip to Venice when they returned with a part of a gondola which is installed in the room. The Stendhal room which is decorated in red and black resulted from the title of his book, Le Rouge et le Noir which they both liked. The theme arose when they found a big black armchair. Marrakech was inspired from their trips to Morocco and the decor is so authentic that guests feel they are in the country.

"Problems arise when a guest checks in and wants the same bedroom but finds it unavailable," she said. "So I suggest why don't you experience another country like

Anne-Christine Meylan

China, Africa or Provence in France. You can travel to different places in our hotel. Or even experience a contemporary style a la mode Philippe Starck, a bedroom which features his mirror."

But the themed decor extends to other rooms. Every year on December 31, she changes the decoration on the ground floor area and last year it was the Orient Express. An artist Nicolas Imhof created large canvases of the interior of the train and the various compartments. On one of the walls in the hotel you will find another secret passion of Anne-Christine Meylan. There is painting of the hotel rising out of the clouds and a biplane with two people.

"I'm lucky because I'm doing a job I like," she said with a charming smile." It's hard work which involves a lot of hours and I'm fortunate because I'm helped by my eldest daughter, Stephanie. But I've the satisfaction of loyalty as about 60% of the customers eat regularly in the restaurant. I take care of them like a doctor takes care of his patients."

Anne-Christine Meylan and Lionel Meylan are a remarkable couple. They each have their separate vocations - he is a watchmaker, and both share a love of flying, going on jaunts in his Dornier biplane. But above all, they have a great sense of fun. Up until 1999, there was only a small quartz clock in the restaurant and one day she glanced up at the wall just below the ceiling in Christopher Bar and discovered a huge sculptural watch which was gift from Lionel. It was made by Michel Emsch, a mechanic of Jean Tinguely.

Jean-Claude Biver

All You Need is Love

Jean-Claude Biver is one of the pioneers and great innovators of the Swiss watch industry. In the hour of crisis, he and Nicolas Hayek senior came up with solutions. Hayek invented the quartz and Biver stood firm with tradition. He brought back Blancpain from extinction by going against the grain with an all-mechanical line when everybody else jumped into quartz.

"It's only when everything goes badly that everyone is interested in something new," he said. It required courage to espouse the slogan, 'Since 1735 there has never been a quartz Blancpain watch and there never will be.'

It took ten years for the company to be launched successfully. But in making such a stand with mechanical watches he has gone down in the history of watch making as someone who single-handedly saved the industry from the quartz movement.

At Swatch, he was asked by Nicolas Hayek senior to help turn around Omega. "We repositioned the brand and brought back its lustre," he said, "through marketing and product placement mainly through James Bond films and celebrity sponsorships by Cindy Crawford, Pierce Brosnan and Michael Schumacher."

Perfect timing

But his greatest contribution to the watch industry was still to come with the young brand Hublot. It was founded in 1980 by Carlo Croco and featured the first natural rubber strap in the history of watch making. Jean-Claude Biver, who was a member of the Swatch Group Directors' Committee, was searching for a new challenge at the same time when Hublot had lost its direction. It was perfect timing!

Biver joined the company in 2004 as CEO and Board member and what he did was to take the idea of fusion outside the envelope. "I married yesterday with tomorrow, the past with the future, tradition with the new," he said. "It was a marriage of gold and rubber. Then gold and ceramics, Kevlar, pink gold or tantalum and rubber - and ultimately the fusion of movements marrying Swiss traditions with 21st century art of watch making."

There is a natural tendency not to look

beyond the commercial success which was incredible with the Big Bang and increased in sales 20 times. But one cannot get away from the fact that what Biver did with Hublot was revolutionary. He launched the mechanical watch like a satellite into an orbit of a new Swiss watch making era. The fusion of unusual materials and styles are endless and can go on ad infinitum.

It begs the question of how was he inspired. "My moment of inspiration came when I saw I.M. Pei's pyramid in the Louvre courtyard," he said. "Here was a perfect example of what I wanted to achieve with Hublot."

Biver was born in Luxembourg on September 20, 1949 and his family moved to Switzerland when he was ten. As a boy he was fascinated by a steam engine and watches - how energy generated could create movement. He was educated at St Prex school, Collège des Morges and the University of Lausanne and arrived in Le Brassus, a village in the Vallèe de Joux, Vaud with a HEC diploma.

It was the cradle of complicated watch making that would mark him for life. He settled near a farm which would later become Blancpain's head office. He started with the prestigious Audemars Piguet and was determined to learn all he could about watch making from the world's best company.

All through his life, he has been guided by the philosophy that has been epitomized by the Beatles song, 'all you need is love.' "If you love someone, you show them respect," he said. "The word love is synonymous with respect. I would not respect myself if I didn't behave with love towards my customers, my suppliers and competitors. I couldn't have an affair with another woman because it would demonstrate a lack of respect for my wife to whom I'd vowed to be faithful in marriage. Above all, it would show a lack of respect for myself which is an anathema."

Moubra lake

Jean-Claude Biver who lives on a farm in Tour de la Peilz has a Chalet in Crans-Montana near the hole no 3 of the golf course. He started skiing in Champery and followed his friends to Crans-Montana.

"It's not Zermatt, Verbier or St Moritz for skiing," he said. "It's a place where you can ski with your father, teenagers or your six year old. Verbier on the other hand is more adapted for multi-purpose skiing. Nowadays, I don't enjoy anymore shooting down the slopes doing 3 km in 3 minutes. I prefer to ski halfway and at 11.30 to sit on a terrace in the sun and enjoy raclette and a Fendant. You can do that in Crans-Montana when you start early. The slopes are in sun and not in the shadow and you avoid crowds which I hate when I ski."

Cindy Crawford

He was at the helm of Omega when the company took over the title sponsor from Canon of the European Masters Tournament. "Up to then the event was regional and had no important golfers or celebrities participating," he said. "We put it on the map because we brought along top personalities and did a lot of PR. I had Cindy Crawford to open the first Omega European Masters Tournament and also invited Ivanna Trump. My brother Marc who headed IMG did his best to promote the event with sportsmen and entertainers who were under contract with the company.

"In the end it was a win-win situation because it was a genius of an idea. It helped to reposition Omega as a top luxury brand and highlighted the Crans-sur-Sierre as the most beautiful mountain golf course in the world."

Besides his business which he looks upon as a hobby, he is also a cheese maker. His cows spend the summer in the alpage where they graze on Alpine meadows full of flowers. The special taste is imparted to the milk and cheese. He produces around five tons, all of which is consumed by family, friends and specific restaurants where he donates the cheese. He refuses payment as he wants to be in total control of the distribution. "I want to be master of my cheese until the last piece," he said. Who knows, Biver might also be thinking of another marriage of rennet from the milk and rubber?

Profession: Student of Life

Pierre Abrezol is a trailblazer and the epitome of Ralph Waldo Emerson's maxim: "Don't follow where the path may lead, go instead where there's no path and leave a trail." Pierre Abrezol is a self-made man who strides over two continents, Australia and Europe. In South Australia and Victoria, he is master of two farms with 36,000 sheep, 2,000 cattle and 3,500 hectares under crops and has the largest organic farm in the southern hemisphere. He ended up there when he married his childhood sweetheart, Sabine. His father-in-law had bought two hobby farms during the cold war because of the threat of nuclear war. When he passed away, he took over the farming business and expanded it. Today, it covers 10,000 hectares. In Switzerland, he has a property portfolio with his wife which includes restaurants and several houses.

In Oz, where everything is far apart - Minimay, one of his farms with a population of 9 is 320 km from Adelaide and 400 km from Melbourne, he feels in an expansion mode because there is a lot of space. In Montreux Riviera, where everything is near, he feels in a contraction mode.

"I tend to spend January and February in Oz after the harvest," he said, "and plan the next cropping. I go back to Australia in June-July because it's the end of the financial year and another trip in September as we've our main shearing then. But when I was appointed president of Promove - a private company which promotes the economy of the Riviera and Lavaux through its offer of free advice and service, I come over earlier. I love the Montreux Riviera and wanted to make a contribution to this lovely area."

Pierre Abrezol who lives in Chexbres had an adventurous youth. He was educated in several private schools because it was not easy for him to settle down. His father, Dr

Raymond Abrezol, who was a renowned sophrologist used him as a guinea pig. He got him to practice the easy physical and mental exercises that lead to a relaxed and healthy body and calm and alert mind. His father learnt sophrology from Professor Caycedo and launched it in Europe and the USA. Later, he was asked to coach the Swiss ski team and other Olympic athletes.

"I benefited from sophrology," he said. "Today, my profession is a student of life. Currently, I'm working on several projects and considering establishing a new foundation, True Values Foundation. One of the projects I'm involved in is the stevia plant which will replace sugar in the near future. It's also suitable for diabetics."

Pierre's first job after gaining his matriculation was in a photographic studio. Later, he worked for Professor Hahn as a photographer before he was asked to learn about prosthetics - constructing artificial hearts. Consequently, he went to Japan to work with professor Tagusi, Hiroshima university and then with professor Bucherl, Charlottenburg hospital, Berlin. When he returned, he was the only person with such a vocation in Switzerland. Then he decided to work for himself and took over Dynaform which sold physiotherapy equipment.

In 1999, he bought a wholesale Aboriginal art company which was based in Brisbane. He still owns some 800 works which includes Johnny Warangkula, Michael Nelson Tjakamarra, Dr George Tjapaltjarri and Emily Kame Kngwarreye, among others.

Pierre Abrezol

"I've never stopped learning and never will," he said. "You must always keep your mind open. My advice is never to let your ego to take over. You can always learn something from anyone irrespective of their vocation in life. Always respect others. Just be who you are and not what you think you are!"

Steady Force

Paul Bulcke is the CEO of Nestlé and was born in Belgium. After he graduated in commercial engineering and management in 1977, he joined the group at the age of 25 and was appointed to the top position in 2008. Under his watch, profits rose to CHF 13.5 billion in 2012 from CHF 12.1 billion in the previous year despite slowing sales. But then he has always been a winner in the sales and profit stakes. When he was entrusted in 2000 with Nestlé's third most important market, Germany, he effected a successful turnaround. Then he took charge of the North and South American markets and under his leadership, they became the group's top regions in terms of sales and profits. He has described Nestlé under his tenure as 'une force tranquille' (a steady force) and is also distinguished by his strong belief in innovation and R & D.

Nestlé's ambition is to enhance the quality of people's lives through nutrition, health and wellness powered by science-based innovation. The company does this through its everyday food and beverage products, systems and services. But Nestlé goes further. It is also expanding the boundaries of nutrition through Nestlé Health Science, which is pioneering ways to address chronic medical conditions through nutrition. With the recent creation of Nestlé Skin Health, the company is expanding the boundaries of health and wellness and entering the field of specialised medical skin treatment. These two companies form two new growth platforms for the Nestlé Group.

"Our success as a company is definitely linked to building more science-based nutritional arguments into our whole portfolio," he said on a visit to the UK where he opened a new bottling plant in Buxton which is part of a £300 million investment. "We have 34 R & D centres round the world including one in Singapore focused on cereals and another in St Louis, Missouri focused on pet care. This is how Nestlé can build the worldwide competency of products which it needs to continue to develop."
"Nestlé is a principles and values based company, " he said. "The way we want to go about our business is through Creating Shared Value. This means that, for a company to be successful over the long term and create value for shareholders, it must also create value for society. We call this Creating Shared Value. We fundamentally believe that our activities should have a positive impact on society, every day, everywhere. To prosper, we have to take a long-term view, framed in a robust set of principles and values that are based on respect for people, respect for the environment, and respect for the world we live in."

Without doubt, he is a shining example of the motto of the Vlerick Leuven Gent Management School where he graduated: **"We don't teach you, we develop what's already inside you."** In 2012, he received the School's VMA award (Management Association, Belgium) for his lifelong career which was distinguished by sustained integrity, exceptional management capacity and inspiring leadership."

In his acceptance speech of the VMA award, Paul Bulcke summarised his job as CEO of Nestlé as follows: "You have to lead things in the right direction, put the right person in the right position and make sure the organisation's values are lived up to explicitly." Leadership in a nutshell!

Prion Reseacher

Professor Dr Andrea Pfeifer who is the CEO of AC Immune and an international expert in Biotech has something in common with her compatriot, Immanuel Kant. It's the predominance of free will which transcends the natural inclinations of man to become an Alpha achiever.

"One day, I sat down with a white piece of paper as there was nothing available on Alzheimers," she said. "But I was determined to proceed. At the time, I was the head of Nestlè's Global research where I managed 600 people. My husband said that if I really wanted to go ahead, he'd support me. My mother thought I was crazy. But after over a decade, we've launched the world's first trial of a vaccine against a protein believed to cause Alzheimer's. Along the way, we even discovered an Andean village, Yarumal, Colombia where the disease strikes younger people in their 40s and inherited a single genetic mutation that guarantees they'll develop it."

Professor Pfeifer who lives with her husband in St. Legier completed her studies and doctoral work in Pharmacy and Pharmacoloy at the University of Würzberg, Germany. She did her postdoctoral in Molecular Carcinogenesis at the National Institutes of Health, Human Carcinogenesis Branch, Bethesda, USA. As she was a registered toxicologist and Pharmacist, she received her habilitation from the University of Lausanne in 2000. She has published over 200 papers and abstracts in leading scientific journals. "I come from a family of engineers

Prof Andrea Pfeifer

and even as a small girl I could adjust engines," she said. "I knew all the models of cars and it caused problems with my boyfriends. I knew more about engines and cars than they did. If there was something certain after my matura, it was that I would study science and medicine because my parents suffered from chronic diseases. I wanted to cure diseases. They were against me going to the US to study cancer but I was happy there. When I returned I joined Nestlé to do research into functional food."

The story of how she became involved in Alzheimers began when four scientists came to see her when she was head of Global research at Nestlè. Among the group were a Nobel and a Lasker prize winner. Their aim was to get support for research into prion diseases such as transmissible spongiform encephalopathies (TSEs). These are a group of progressive neurodegenerative conditions that effect both humans and animals - Creutzfeldt-Jakob disease (CJD) and bovine spongiform encephalopathy (BSE), Mad cow disease.

"I was impressed by the group's presentation to seek venture funding," she said, "but the number of people

suffering from the disease was nothing in comparison to Alzheimers also caused by a protein particle. We're talking about 1 million compared to 36 million. So we turned them down and suggested they concentrate on Alzheimers. They disagreed and left." She smiled. "They returned later and were interested in changing their research focus. Now I was in a bind because I didn't think that Nestlé would consider such a research proposition."
It was a defining moment of her life. She felt tempted to join the group but it would mean leaving a secure senior management position with an international reputation in nutrition. She had led the development of the first functional food LC1 and one of the first Cosmoceutical products in a joint venture with L'Oreal, Inéovy Fermeté. In addition, she had co-founded the Nestlé Venture Capital Fund, a € 100 million Life Sciences corporate venture fund. But she has never looked back.
"My life changed radically when I accepted the biggest challenge in my life," she said. "In 2003, I became CEO of AC Immune which I co-founded and identifies and develops the 'best in class' innovative therapies for Alzheimer's disease. Contemporaneously, I was appointed chairwoman of the Biotechmedinvest AG Investment Fund which is a dedicated health-care venture capital fund. I also support the AB2Bio company as Chairwoman which is a breakthrough drug discovery and development company focused on establishing leadership in the treatment of inflammatory diseases."

Both companies are located in the EPFL innovation park biocluster together with 230 other biotech companies. Pierre Bottinelli, a top financier, who is one of the investors in Biotechmedinvest has had many years experience with pharmaceutical companies. "I find Professor Pfeifer's research programme has excellent prospects. She's in the mould of another pioneer, Dr Alejandro Zaffaroni, who founded several successful biotechnology companies in Silicone Valley."

"We attract the best candidates and I'm a role model and coach for 50 scientists," she said. "We have some 60% women on our staff and the new generation doesn't have it as tough as I had. They manage a family as well as a top career which they feel they deserve by virtue of their ability and talent. We have no glass ceilings in our companies. Today, the biggest health concerns are cardiology and cancer but tomorrow it will be Alzheimer's and inflammation."

Over the past 15 years, some 100 experimental Alzheimer drugs have failed in tests to either modify or slow the progression of the disease. AC Immune's vaccine ACI-35 aims to stimulate the body's immune system to produce antibodies to target the tau protein that forms twisted fibres and tangles inside the brain. There is still no treatment which can modify or slow the progression of the disease. In her quest, Professor Pfeifer never hesitated to change her roles from top biotech scientist to heading a venture capital fund to achieve her goals. If there is anyone who deserves to discover the effective drug it should be her. But then she would be a big winner not only for the sufferers of this terrible disease but also for her longstanding investors. Industry investors estimate that the market is worth $10 billion in annual sales.

Smoke over the Water

Michel Ferla who was born in Vevey and lived in Corseaux is a tourism expert par excellence. His two mentors, Raymond Jaussi and Claude Nobs were both visionaries and had a crucial impact on tourism in Montreux. Raymond Jaussi, director of Montreux Tourism Office, saw the first BBC television transmission in 1929 and organised the television transmission of the Narcissus festival in Montreux in 1954, together with Swiss Television.

"Jaussi and Claude Nobs later hired me to work for Montreux Tourism," said Michel Ferla who became Director of the Montreux Tourism Office in 1980. "Claude had already organised many evening concerts for the Rose d'Or with groups like Hair, the Rolling Stones, among others. In 1967, he established the Montreux Jazz and invited many renowned artists such as Aretha Franklin, Roberta Flack to perform. Today more than 6000 hours of music have been recorded of the live performances of the Montreux Jazz Festival. Probably the largest archives of music in the world."

He recalled the famous incident in 1971 when the casino caught fire. Frank Zappa and the Mothers of Invention were on stage. Someone shot a flare gun and the top corner of the hall caught fire. Very soon the place was alight and there was a danger of pandemonium as people began to panic. Frank Zappa stopped the band and took control of the situation. He talked them out safely. Some children had run into the kitchen and down the stairs to a dead end and Claude Nobs rescued them and took them to safety. Later, Deep Purple sat in the restaurant of the hotel Eden du Lac and watched the flames racing into the sky as the casino burnt to the ground. Ian Gillen of the band watched smoke drift over lake Geneva and was inspired to write the Smoke over the water, one of the famous rock songs of the 1970s.

"Another piece of music memorabilia is in the new casino," said Michel Ferla who is the president of the foundation of the Casino Barrière Montreux. "There's an exhibition called Queen -The Studio Experience which charts the band's association with the studios, their personal relationship with Montreux and the seven albums which were written and recorded there from 1978-1996 including the final one, Made in Heaven. We're proud to show how Queen contributed to the cultural musical heritage of the town."

After 15 years as the Director of the Montreux Tourist Office, he joined Switzerland tourism in 1996. His first posting was in Paris and then in Zurich at the headquarters. He was given the responsibility of opening up emerging markets in Russia, India, Korea P.R., China and the Middle East. He also supervised the markets such as Japan and South East Asia and participated in the creation of the Switzerland Destination

Management (now named the Switzerland Travel Centre). In 2000, he was appointed Vice Director of Swiss Tourism. Three years later, he assumed responsibility for France, Belgium and Spain in which he opened an office in Barcelona. In France, he had several successful campaigns linked to the theme 'vacation of the year.'

"We offered two French swimmers to spend their rest periods in Switzerland, before the London Olympics as guests of Switzerland "The land of water," said Michel. "Camille Muffat and Yannick Agnel became both three-time Olympic medalists. Their testimonials were great. So we based our tourism campaign in France."

In India, Switzerland became the set for Bollywood actors and producers, thanks to its resemblance to the Kashmir region. It was also due to the kindness of a Gstaad taxi driver and service providers in Switzerland. Today, Switzerland is second to the UK as the most popular country for Indian tourists to visit in Europe.

"If I was asked about choosing staff I would repeat what I was once told by the chairman of Club Mediterranean," he said. "I look at people's eyes and when they shine then I know they're right. Such eyes show enthusiasm and passion. My favourite places in Switzerland include Kandersteg where you can walk on path that takes you back 200 years and obviously the Montreux Riviera. For Montreux, I would suggest a walk along the promenade from the Excelsior hotel towards Montreux during mid April to early July because of the scented trees and flowers. In terms of sightseeing, my advice is to see Chillon castle, take the cogwheel railway up to Rochers de Naye, cruise on lake Geneva which is the largest in Europe, visit Lavaux vineyards (Unesco world Heritage site) lunch at the Auberge de l'Onde which is situated in a beautiful historic house in St Saphorin and finally, don't miss Vevey's Saturday market and its "marché folklorique" in the summer."

Watchmaker Needs Good Knees

Lionel Meylan's family has had strong ties with the Swiss watchmaking tradition for six generations. Although, there are documents in which the family is mentioned in 1386, their origins are in the valley de Joux. The watchmaking industry was established there as well as in La Chaux de Fonds which are both in the Jura.

"I remember my grandfather's studio when I was a little boy and I was allowed to unscrew and then screw together an old alarm clock," he said. "My confirmation present at 16 was a Fludo which was a 20th century brand made in the village of les Breuleux by Fluvius Boillot. The workshop which was called a cabinet was under a master. It was usually located in the top floor of a house where there was most light. From the beginning of watchmaking there were three categories in the workshop. The people making specialised components. Those who bought components and others who assembled watch components. On average about 90% of the components were made in-house. The brand name was put on the dial and watches were sold all over the world from these small workshops."

Then he smiled. "There could be variations on these categories. The situation exists even today and you find some brands like Rolex and Jaeger-Lecoultre who make everything in- house and others like Cartier, Vacheron Constantin and Baume & Mercier are assembling manufacturers."

When Lionel graduated from a watchmaking school, it was the crisis in the watch industry because of the invention of the electronic watch. Suddenly, there was no need for mechanical watches. There was still work in maintaining clocks both public and private. Lionel then went to commercial school and began to work in his own apartment. His grandfather would send him watches to repair and service.

"There have been many developments in the history of watchmaking from the pocket watch to the wristwatch," he said. "One of the earliest pioneers was A.L. Bréguet (1747-1823) who was responsible for several developments. He created the self-winding perpetual watch, the first carriage clock for Napoleon (1801) and the world's first wristwatch for the Queen of Naples, Caroline Murat (1810). Another breakthrough was the introduction of the Reverso watch by Jaeger-Lecoultre. Polo-playing British officers in India often broke the crystal glass face during competitions and this led to the development of the first sports watch. The glass face could twist completely round so that it could be protected by a steel case." There are 40 different professions involved in watchmaking. From the draughtsman, the concept of the mechanics - either simple or complicated, the design, the prototype to the design of the case, the dial, the hands, the crown and ultimately the production. But the watchmaker is a totally different breed from the ordinary person.

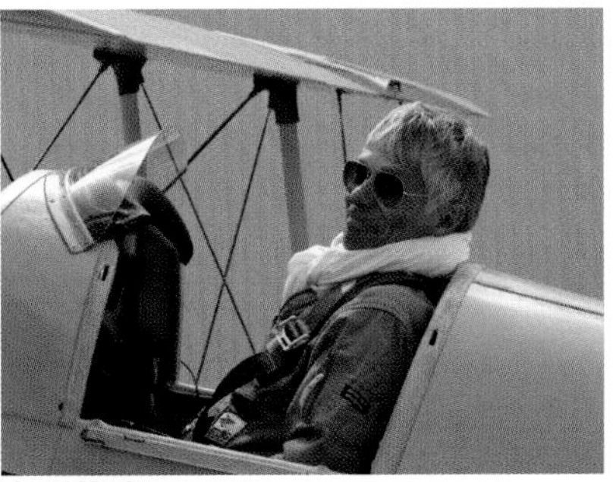

Lionel Meylan

"He needs precision in his fingers, an angel's patience, good eyes and nerves of steel," said Lionel. Then he laughed. "But above all, good knees. When a component drops onto the floor, you need to find it. So you're on knees crawling for a long time with a little brush. Above all, the watchmaker needs a taste for challenge in servicing. It's not the money that drives him but to find a good solution. He receives a watch in poor condition and is required to return it in good condition."

Lionel Meylan's other passion is flying. It began when he was a child of three and his father took him on a flight in a Piper cub two-seater whilst he sat on his father's knees. His passion never stopped and while other boys were into cars, he was into planes, drawing pictures of them and assembling plastic and balsa wood models of them.

"I even had a plane with a benzine engine," he said. "This was before a remote control and it tended to nosedive and damage the fuselage. So I learnt to repair the models. And then I became interested in gliders in 1977 and learnt to fly them at Bex. It gave me a tremendous feeling of freedom and I got to know about winds and how to use the thermals. I obtained all the different glider licenses from single operation to passenger, aerobatic and finally cloud license which allowed the pilot to conduct instrument flying. In 1984, I gained my glider instructors license."

Dornier bi-plane

Parallel to gliding activities, Lionel Meylan obtained his private pilot's license for a single engine piston aircraft at Lausanne. He began towing gliders in an effort to gain more flying experience. By this time, he had met Christine and he invited her for a flight in a glider.

"Fortunately, she liked the idea of flying," he said and smiled. "But she's quite small and I had to make special shoes which would lengthen her feet to operate the rudder. I'm fortunate as many of my pilot friends fly alone as their wives don't like taking to the air. She often accompanies me on my flights in the Dornier bi-plane too."

Although, it's not obvious there is a connection between watchmaking and flying. At the beginning of aircraft development, there was a need to control and navigate by instruments alone i.e. instrument flying. The watchmaking industry was in a good position to provide the necessary equipment. Lionel flies under instrument rules with a commercial pilot license and uses his knowledge whenever visual conditions are not safe. If you reached 200 feet from the ground without visibility then you have to abort the landing and start again.

"In those early days, pilots navigated along the iron road - the railway lines," he said, "and once they reached a landmark such as a junction they started the stopwatch and headed 030 degrees for seven minutes, for example, before they reached another landmark such as the first chimney of the village. Timing as well as the compass was the only way to navigate. If you reached 200ft from the ground without visibility then you had to abort the landing and start again."

Lionel Meylan who is an experienced pilot has already had three engine failures in his twin engined aircraft. It requires flying at full power on the other engine and set the balance to fly straight ahead.

"The aircraft flies quite well but a little slower," he said, "and you have to request an emergency landing at the nearest airport."

Both he and his wife enjoy their flights and have even travelled to islands like Corsica.

First Nestle Powder Milk Baby

Pierre Aguet who was born in Vevey has an innate love of the city. In his retirement, he enjoys showing visitors all the nooks and crannies of the place. There are the underground cellars and rooms where the municipal wine is made and where the city fathers can taste the vintages. Then he points out the first house, Maison de l'Almanach du messager Boiteux which was built in 1740 and is at the beginning of the rue du Lac. The next site is Place du Marché which is dominated by the Grenette which is a Neoclassical rustic style of 1803. But what he is most proud of is another building - a row of terraced wooden houses which he had built during his term on the city council.

"I started out as a postman but after obtaining a degree in Administration in Lausanne," he said, "and at 32 years old I became a professional politician, secretary of the Socialist party. I have been a member of the city council for 17 years and then on the government of the Vevey for 18 years. After 12 years at the Vaud cantonal parliament I became a member of the national council and was one of the delegates was also a delegate from who prepared the text on humanitarian rights and law that applied to the Geneva Convention. One of my last acts was to sign a cheque for CHF 50 million to renovate SATOM which is the waste incinerator for Vaud and the Valais cantons."

Pierre Aguet

Another source of pride is that he persuaded Nestlé when they built their HQ to donate the lower part of their grounds to the city. This would give the public access to the lakeshore and the city would provide funds to landscape the land. But his link with the company began at birth because his mother died afterwards. He was one of the first milk powder babies who was brought in Nestlé's nursery. Before the company launched their product, Lactogen, they tested it on babies and Pierre Aguet was one of the babies chosen. He has flourished since then on the breast milk substitute and has made a big contribution to the quality of life of Vevey.

2

Julie Enckell Juliard ©Viktoria Bosc

Museums and Art Galleries

Jenisch Museum

Avenue de la Gare 2
Tel 021 925 3520
info@museejenisch.ch
www.museejenisch.ch

Closed Mondays.
Open late until 9 pm on Thursday.

The Jenisch is a gallery of fine arts that hosts the Cantonal print room. It is an architectural gem of a gallery and a great discovery. Jenisch's selection although small, has several seminal works from renowned artists: Albrecht Dürer, Pablo Picasso, Marcel Duchamp, Gustave

Gustave Courbet Coucher de Soleil

Courbet, Pierre Bonnard and the Swiss painters like Ferdinand Hodler, Ernest Biéler and Félix Vallotton. It also houses the works of the Oskar Kokoschka foundation and has a print room with over 30,000 prints and 5,000 drawings from the Renaissance to the present day. Some of the engravings include Rembrandt, Lorrain, Canaletto, Corot and Degas. Outstanding examples include Annibale Carracci, Giovanni Andrea De Ferrari or Tiepolo. (See entry Dominique Radrizzani)

"We are fortunate as we have a unique and fascinating collection," said Julie Enckell Julliard, director of the Jenisch Museum. "What's also of interest is the building itself which was built in a neoclassical style by architects Louis Maillard and Robert Convert in 1897. It's suited to displaying works because of its spaciousness and light."

In keeping with the building's style, a replica of the Parthenon frieze adorns its façade while the entrance hall and main staircase have mosaic floors and are decorated with columns and statues based on models from antiquity. But a colourful welcome is given in the reception hall by the two murals of Ernst Biéler which were executed in 1922. These huge frescos were preceded by another work in Vevey, the windows at the church of St Martin.

"I am particularly proud of Gustave Courbet's and Ferdinand Hodler's works in our collection," she said. "They are masterpieces. Courbet painted his house in La Tour de Peilz and a magnificent view from it onto the lake. In a letter to Whistler, he remarked on the gigantic mountains and the horizon. The portrait of Max Buchon in 1855 reminds me of Manet's Le Joueur de Fifre which was painted later in 1866. Both figures have the same stance and construction. Hodler's Eiger, Mönch and Jungfrau is exciting because you can see the beginnings of the abstract landscapes in 1908."

Other highlights include Félix Vallotton, Rochers à mare basse 1917 which features a pile of rocks and a blocked horizon; an early Picasso painted when he was only 18; and the Kokoschka collection. There are only two places in the world where you can study his work, in Vienna and Vevey. The Kokoschka foundation moved here because it is where he spent the last 25 years of his life. His works which are an example of German Expressionism emphasise depth perception. "A landscape can be described only on a objective basis," he said. "It can't be fixed by a camera. It can't be painted as 'nature morte'. A landscape is also something living... this is what I've been trying to realise in a painting."

A room is devoted the avant-garde movement Cobra art, a name which was derived from the artists' home cities - Copenhagen, Brussels and Amsterdam. Works of one of the founders, Asger Jorn, and a member, Alex Alechinsky, are exhibited.

Another interesting work is by Marcel Duchamp, Piston de courant d'air (Piston of drafts of air) 1914 and is a good example of conceptual art. A piece of gauze netting in front of a window recorded the changes in the nettings shape in response to the warm currents of air from the radiator below. There is an anecdote about his holiday which he spent with Mary Reynolds at Chexbres and Chardonne. While in the area, he found a waterfall which he had been looking for all his life. It is called the Forestay's Brook which can today be seen from the car park at Hotel Baron Tavernier and falls into lake Geneva at Rivaz. It later became a principal element, after a period of 20 years of reflection, of his last masterpiece Etant donnés. (See entry Duchamp).

A popular work in the print section is the Dürer's Melancholia. It's one of the most famous old master prints. The dark temperament is personified by a female winged figure seated in the foreground. From her belt hang keys and a money bag which symbolise power and wealth. The winged infant beside her is a genius.

The Jenisch was established in 1897, through to a legacy of 200,000 francs from Fanny Henriette Jenisch (1801–1881), wife of Martin Johan Jenisch, a senator of Hamburg who came to live in Vevey. It is the second largest art museum in Vaud and has a viewing room, the Leenaards hall, on the top of the building which offers good conditions for examining works on paper. It contains an extensive library and archival holdings. The viewing room is available by appointment.

Julie Enckell Julliard, the director, who is an art historian and lives Pully studied in Lausanne, Rome and Paris. She has doctorate on Medieval Italian art and a postgraduate degree from Geneva University Art and Design (HEAD). Her first position was at Jenisch Museum when she was appointed curator of modern and contemporary art. Julie has written several articles about artists as well as on the usage of paper in contemporary art. She was appointed director in 2013 and has introduced an ambitious programme.

"My aim at Jenisch is to develop the museum as a living and open space," she said. "In increasingly digital world, the team at the museum both shapes and fosters research as well as promoting art on paper."

The museum has a lively programme of events from vernissages to finissages, brunch and visits to other museums. There are three exhibitions a year. One of the recent shows included the first solo exhibition of Manon Bellet, who was born in Vevey in 1979 and lives and works in Berlin. Besides her monumental installations, serial works and videos, she has a special interest in paper. Opaque or transparent, crumpled or torn, gradually disintegrated by fire or fluttering in a draft, the page moves and transforms itself in the artist's hands as she sets out to explore the potential new lives. Of particular note is a catalogue on a multidisciplinary exhibition called Lemancolia which was organised by the former director, Dominiqe Radrizzani. It is a pity the publication is only in French.

Villa "Le Lac" Le Corbusier

Route de Lavaux 21
1802 Corseaux
079 829 63 08
lecorbusier@villalelac.ch
www.villalelac.ch

The small museum of Le Corbusier is a 'must see' for aficionados of architecture as well as tourists who want to experience the best view of lake Geneva from the Swiss Riviera. The ribbon window allows for the capture of the exterior into the inner space. The view is comparable to Ferdinand Hodler's paintings of the panoramic view of the lake and Mont Blanc which was painted from his apartment in Geneva.

Le Corbusier Villa "Le Lac"

The great architect built the Maison Blanche in 1912 for his parents in his birthplace La Chaux-de-Fonds. When it was sold in 1919, he embarked on a mission to design another house for them. His search covered the years 1922-23 and involved trips on the Paris- Milan and Orient Express (Paris-Ankara).

"In my pocket was the plan of a house," said Le Corbursier. "A plan without a site? The plan of a house in search of a plot of ground? Yes!"

He found the site in Corseaux on chemin Bèrgere, an almost deserted track, an old Roman road which linked the diocese of Sion in the Valais with Lausanne and Geneva. The plot which was on the shore of lake Geneva had a stunning view and

2

was built in 1923-4 by Le Corbusier and his cousin, Pierre Jeanneret, also an architect with whom he collaborated. His parents moved into the Villa Le Lac in 1924 and his father, Georges Edouard Jeanneret, died a year later while his mother, Marie Charlotte Amélie Jeanneret-Perret lived there until her 100th year. After her death in 1960, Albert Jeanneret, Le Corbusier's brother stayed there alone until he died in 1973.

"The house prefigures three of the five points of the new architecture," said Patrick Moser, the curator of Villa "Le Lac". "The use of the roof as a sun deck or garden, the open plan and the ribbon window. It's a machine for living. It's the place where you can find the key ideas for his famous white houses. In fact from 1924 to 1951, it served as a laboratory for his concepts. What's remarkable is his use of space and although, it's only 64 m2, you get the impression of a much larger overall area."

Patrick Moser has become a prime interpreter of Le Corbusier's work much in the same way as Robert Craft was for Stravinsky. The story began when Patrick wanted to become a curator of MOMA in New York. He gained his masters as an art historian on British landscape painting of ruins of 18th/19th century. He followed with a DPDS in museology and applied to MOMA for a job but they said he should have work experience first. Patrick worked for six months at the historical museum in Geneva. Then MOMA dismissed his job application again because it was unpaid work.

"I finally landed up at the Villa "Le Lac" in 1999 when I replaced an old lady who opened up the door once a week on Wednesday afternoon," he said with a smile. "I've never left since and during my period here I've greatly appreciated the functionality, the harmony and the nuances of Le Corbusier's work. I'm proud that I run the smallest museum in the Montreux Riviera. Tourists visit other museums because they are in the region but in our case they come to the region just to visit us."

The house as it stands today has remained true to the original plan. An upper annex was added on the northwest in 1931 to house Le Corbusier and his wife, Yvonne Gallis, when they came to stay. It was a small space of 10 m2 which contained a bunk bed and a platform for a chair and a desk. When he sat at the desk he could see the lake through a ribbon window. The north facades were surfaced with hot-dip galvanised sheets in the same year and the wall that closes off the property on the north side was added when the a road was built to replace chemin Bèrgere. In 1962, the Villa "Le Lac" became a grade 1 listed building and 22 years later was opened to the public. It became a museum in 2010, about 11 years after Patrick became a door opener.

"A wonderful addition to the museum was when Nicole Beuchat joined," he said. "She's a graphic designer who has worked with architects. Nicole not only created the website but designed the elegant series of catalogues of our exhibitions. Two of them can be considered as collectors' items. The catalogue devoted to Erling Mandelmann, the photographer who shot a series of interiors in black and white during 1964-5 when Albert Jeanneret lived there. Another photographer, René Burri, who achieved fame by taking the photo of Che Gevara smoking a cigar, created a fascinating exhibition of intimate photos of Le Corbusier. He was fortunate as he became a chronicler of Le Corbusier's day-to-day activities. Once he was castigated by the master as he was rash enough to take a photo which seemed to show Le Corbusier praying before a painting."

Nicole like Patrick was drawn to the Villa "Le Lac".The first time she was brought by her boyfriend and the next time, she brought another boyfriend to see it. On the third occasion she was surprised to find a man who opened the door and not an old lady.

"The Villa reminds me of my grandparents home in the Jura," she said. "It's modest too but there's a magical quality to it. There's an impression of spaciousness and I love the picture window of the concrete wall in the garden with two benches side by side."

In 2013, the Villa "Le Lac" was featured at MOMA in an exhibition, Le Corbusier: An Atlas of Modern Landscapes. No one was more delighted than Patrick Moser for it was a complete circle. MOMA had accepted him at last.

Alimentarium Food Museum

Quai Perdonnet 25
1800 Vevey
Tel 021 9244111
www.alimentarium.ch

The Alimentarium is the world's first museum devoted to man and his food. It has a permanent exhibition on two floors which highlights the four stages of food from cultivation to assimilation in the body. An 8-metre stainless steel fork stuck in lake Geneva just outside marks its location.

"The museum is a historic building and housed the first administrative offices of Nestlé in 1920," said Ursula Zeller, the director. "Besides one original room which has been devoted to Henri Nestlé and the story of the company, the ultra modern kitchen offers food workshops for both adults and children. It is one of the most popular museums in Switzerland and has had 1.5 million visitors."

One of its best kept secrets is the restaurant La Verrière which is located in the bright conservatory with fragrant citrus aromas of hanging plants. The menus which vary monthly and are called 'voyages of discovery' cover cuisines from Japan, Iran,Vietnam, Switzerland and the Mediterranean.

"A radical change is on the way as the Alimentarium will reinvent itself," she said. "In future, two thirds will be web-based and digital for worldwide audiences and only a third with be physical and part of the museum. The magazine on our website is a start.

It'll be a combination of learning centre and museum."

Vevey Castle museums

History Museum

rue du Chateau 2
Tel 021 925 5164
musee.historique@vevey.ch
www.museehistoquevevey.ch

Vevey Castle which is a fine example of 16th century Bernese architecture. The building of the castle with its huge roof almost the same size as the building was once the residence of the Bernese bailiffs. The museum comprises a diverse collection of furniture, ancient weapons, medals, engravings, manuscripts and Swiss paintings as well as a unique collection of keys, locks and ancient caskets.

Brotherhood of Winegrowers Confrérie des Vignerons Museum

rue du Chateau 2
Vevey
Tel 021 923 8705
confrerie@fetedesvignerons.ch
www.fetedesvignerons.ch
Open from Tuesday to Sunday 11am to 5 pm.

The office and archives open on Monday, Tuesday and Thursday in the mornings from 8.30 to 11.45.

The museum contains the history of one of the most unique festivals in the world which began in the 17th century. It's devoted to the humungous event of

Ernest Bieler Les Vendanges 1905 Fetes des Vignerons

the Fête des Vignerons and the pageant celebrates in music, costumes and dance the region's viticulture. Videos of the spectacular earlier festivals are shown. Sabine Carruzzo-Frey is the secretary and is the author of Du labeur aux honneurs which is the history of the Winegrowers Festival with lavish illustrations. (See entry François Margot, Events and Brasserie La Couple)

Morgan Art Gallery

Rue du Théatrè 9 Vevey
Tel 079 2787799
valerie@morgan-art.ch
www.morgan-art.ch

Charles Morgan is a Swiss artist known for his sculptural machines. But he wears his creative mantle lightly with a sense of humour and it's easy to dismiss his work as Heath Robinson contraptions - ridiculously complicated machines for achieving simple objectives.

"I came to Switzerland as a 13 year-old when my father who was a graphic designer was headhunted for Nestlé," he said. "My ultimate dream then was to become an artist like Tinguely. But not so sad and tragic. Fancy building something that would self-destruct. Maybe he had problems with his Dada."

The dream was realised in a roundabout way. At home, he was encouraged in his creative activities which consisted of visiting the local tip and turning bits of metal into objects like jewellery. He had a penchant for metal in all its shapes and varieties. Later, when he applied for art school he was rejected because of his poor French.

"Instead, I did an apprenticeship as a goldsmith in Lausanne," he said. "At the same time, I studied the principles of machines, electricity, electronics and other modern technologies like laser. When I completed my four-year apprenticeship, I opened a jewellery shop in Vevey."

His designs were extraordinary to say the least. Rings with secret compartments, pendants that could be opened in 12 different ways, jewels electronically controlled and cigarette lighter cases like small steam locomotives. But his talent as a craftsman burst forth and one day, he made a work titled, The Tonsils, which he put in the window. Within a short time, he had sold it and he was launched on his artistic career in 1974.

"I called it tonsils because I was suffering from tonsillitis," he said with a laugh. "A German tourist saw it in the window and wanted to buy it immediately. But I wasn't happy as the motor was unreliable. So I told him to come back in a couple of weeks. He asked me to do the work in a green and blue colour." Another laugh. "Later, he became my father-in-law."

He has never looked back. He has undertaken 15 major commissions including two for the Swiss government - Tourismusflipper and Switzerball, as well as for Nestlé and Samsung. But what has eluded him has been artistic recognition. Like Tinguely, his work is made from everyday objects, pieces of scrap or junk

Charlie Morgan

and is of a mechanical nature, serving no purpose except the motor which drives the metal parts in a smooth movement like the cyclist or downward movement of a ball that triggers other components. But he has created an unconventional beauty in the knock-on effect of different components and in the use of bicycle wheels, vehicle parts and industrial offal in the sculptures.

"I'm happiest when I go shopping for metal objects in my Aladdin's cave under my workshop," he said. "I like to start a new project that way. It's like liquorice allsorts because it gets my creative juices flowing. For autumn and summer in the Four Seasons - a quadtych, I used artificial flowers which I bought in Kiev - the Ukrainians put them on gravestones. In the Lead Lady, the breasts were made from colander bowls which I found on a dump and a plastic surgeon provided me with silicone pad for one of the breasts."

The workshop was a lucky happenstance for Morgan. One day, he passed a workshop to let in Jongny on Philippe Meylan's estate. But he found that several people were already interested. Later, he met the Meylan's at his exhibition and they rang the next day to say that he could have it. But before he agreed, he spent the night there with his five year old son. They slept well and woke up surrounded by a mist and cows. It was perfect.

"My latest toy, is a Raspberry Pi," he said with a board smile. "It's a credit-sized single- board computer. I'm figuring out how I can incorporate it in my sculptural machines."

But there is more than meets the eye with Morgan. One would think that his sculptural machines should be in galleries and museums worldwide. After all, he has created some 2,000 during his 35 year career and some of his largest works have been bought by Switzerland tourism and Samsung. The reason is that he is fiercely independent and as he resented the high commission of gallerists, he established his own gallery.

"Charlie, is an artist cum craftsman," said Marie-Claire 'Mali' Morgan, a chic woman and former wife."When we were together in the 1980's, he never stopped working from day to night. In the morning, he would tell me of his dreams and then express them in his work. Although he is a jeweller, he treats plastic the same as precious stones. He creates a magic world and at the same time, de-dramatises art. Unlike Tinguely whose art is dark and destructive, Charlie's is funny - he has a great sense of humour, and appeals to children as well."

Swiss Camera Museum

Place du Marché
Vevey
Tel 021 925 3480
cameramuseum@vevey.ch
www.cameramuseum.ch

Open Tuesday-Sunday. 11 am to 5.30 pm.

Over five floors, this museum exhibits the inventors and techniques of the world of photography throughout the ages. The permanent exhibition ranges from camerae obscurae to the most up-to-date digital cameras. The five sections include the beginnings of photography, the plate era, the century of film, the digital revolution and magic lanterns.

In addition, there are several camera types on display such as Leica, Kodak, Sinar and Alpha. What makes the museum unique are the treasures from photographic history: Hans Finsler's Rolleiflex, Hermann Koenig's Leica, Gertude Fehr's Sinar and Robert Frank's little Leica used to shoot the iconoclastic 1958 book, The Americans. Frank received a Guggenheim grant for the project and spent 1955 and 1956 on the road in the US, often living among his subjects while he photographed them. He took some 28,000 photos of which only 83 were chosen for the book.

There are also interactive installations, animations, games, videos and books mainly intended for young visitors. Throughout the year temporary exhibitions complement the permanent one.

2

Chaplin's World: The Modern Museum Times Museum

The multi-million pound Chaplin Museum dedicated to the life of the silent screen star will open in Spring in 2016. It will be in his former home, the Manoir de Ban in Corsier-sur- Vevey, a 350-acre estate in the heart of the Swiss Riviera where he spent the last 25 years of his life. The museum has the blessing of his children whose close cooperation made the project possible.

Nestlé Centre

Walt Disney's heritage is Disneyland and now Henri Nestlé too will have his constructed environment and prescribed visitor experience. The giant food company is planning to open a Nestlé Visitor Centre in June 2016.

Shops

Lionel Meylan

Watchmaker-Jeweller

Place du Marché 4
Rue des Deux-Marchés 14
Vevey
Tel 021 925 5050
info@lionel-meylan.ch
www.lionel-meylan

For generations, the Meylan family have cultivated a watchmaking tradition and expertise which unique in Switzerland. At their shops in Vevey, Lionel Meylan brings together the most outstanding watches from 14 prestigious brands and 11 jewellery companies. Apart from the exceptional collections, the company offers its clients expert service and personalised advice about watches and jewellery.

There is another feature to Lionel Meylan. He offers a masterclass in watchmaking. Over three hours you get to know how to take a watch apart and put it together again. Each person is given eight professional tools including a loupe and you are shown how to handle them. It's fun and hard work but logical. When the tiny bits of metal and rubies come together, one feels a sense of achievement. Meylan's pleasant personality has made the going easy and students feel in his presence that they are part of the DNA of 500 years of watchmaking. The cost is CHF 300 per person and a maximum of four in a group

The ultimate in the masterclass is to have your own branded watch. This is done in two stages. The first is to select the case, the dial and the design. The second is the assembly of the watch which can take a day. The cost to make your own handmade watch with your name on the dial is from CHF 1,200. The venue for the masterclass is in Rue des Marchés 34 which is opposite the other shop at Rue des Deux-Marchés 14.

"Watches are not only instruments to give time," said Lionel Meylan, "they also serve as status symbols as well as works of art. Watches are also given to commemorate special events like confirmation, anniversaries or birthdays. For me, a watch represents a great emotion of the history of watchmaking and the heritage of our country."

L'air du Temps

Rue des deux Marchés Vevey
Tel 021 922 2303
lairdutemps@bluewin.ch
www.lairdutemps.ch
shop.lairdutemps.ch

If you only have enough time to visit one shop in Vevey, then it should be L'air du Temps. It is a cave of delights and full of surprises. Michelin chefs will be floored by the 260 spices that can be used in their dishes. English people will be shocked to the core to find that tea which is not only their cultural beverage but also of the French. They can discover Paris breakfast tea, four types of Earl Grey and a famous tea firm, Mariage Frères (MF), which rivals Twinings and Jacksons of Piccadilly. Wine buffs will be amazed by the number of accoutrement in stock. Besides, the

Riedel selection of glasses for different wines, sabres to slash off the champagne corks, there are glass markers of different colours and shapes which sit on the rim of the glass to distinguish one guest from another.

The man behind it all is Luc Beldi who lives in Montreux. His early background was in the kitchen of his mother who was a good cook. He began travelling extensively to destinations such as Canada where he spent six months, San Francisco, Thailand and China.

"The concept for the cave of delights came during my travels," he said, "and my hobby has always been the kitchen. I enjoyed spending time there, making different types of desserts. Then I worked as a buyer for Mövenpick shops for 11 years. It gave a me a wide experience of foods from ice cream, salmon, coffee, tea, boulangerie among other products, before I opened L'Air du Temps."

Essentially, the shop is an epicerie fine or delicatessen and its heart is the tea section. It is there in the middle on two sides of the counter where you will find a glorious selection of 122 loose teas and another 100 in boxes. The categories comprise green, black, blue, white and the only red, rooibos:Mariage Frères reigns supreme.

Among the Second Flush:Summer harvest teas, is the king of black Darjeeling tea, the famous Castleton estate which produces a chestnut coloured liquor with its distinctive taste of muscatel (T1110). And alongside it (T1109) is the

Luc Beldi

'Himalayan Mists', created specially for MF. The prestigious black tea produced in the misty mountains of Darjeeling is composed solely of silvery buds. Selective plucking occurs only in the coolness of an evening under a rising moon. The young, downy leaves produce a golden liquor tasting of hazelnut and muscatel with a floral aroma. Opposite the tea counter are the range of teapots from Japanese ironware to terracotta.

"I'm fortunate in that I have a good memory for the tastes of most teas," he said with a smile, "but I also like coffee. I have a special brand which is roasted in La Chaux de fonds. It's La Semeuse, a grand cru."

The front of the shop is for the sweet-toothed. The shelves are packed with biscuits, honey, chocolates - an innovation is la Douceur des Fees with absinthe, jams including the queen of confiture, Christine Ferber, with her classic blueberry and raspberry with star anise. Next is the vast selection of spices which merit close inspection because of the many surprises like black truffle salt and wasabi root. Once you are past the teas you enter the realm of the knives. Here specialities include the ceramic knife and the panoramic knives in which the cutting edge is shaped into outlines of famous mountain ranges such as the Matterhorn and the Mont Blanc.

L'air du Temps is a good source of presents for every occasion. An unmissable experience for every age and every taste from gourmands to unseasoned cooks. Surely, the best present is the MF book, The French Art of Tea. It will be an appropriate present to a Brit!

Boutique 6éme Sens

Rue du lac 30
Vevey
Tel 021 921 7004

Jackie Kennedy's fashion heritage is alive and well in this small boutique. The clothes are elegant, chic and sober from ready-to-wear ranges with fitting accessories. Dominique Miserez who owns the boutique has fashion at her fingertips. It is her sixth sense as the name of the shop denotes.

Altmann Sports

Rue de la Madeleine 22
Vevey
Tel 021 921 9677
info@altmannsports.ch
www.altmannsports.ch

Altmann Sports is one of the best sport shops in the Swiss Riviera. It not only has a comprehensive range of equipment but also it stocks the latest innovations. From climbing, skiing, ski touring, snowboarding, trekking, skating, biking to tennis, badminton, swimming, clothing and all the accessories to go with the activities, can be found here.

"I'm proud of the service we can offer clients whether they buy or rent," said François De Crousaz, the owner who lives in Blonay. "Besides the repair and maintenance of bikes, skis and snowboards, we also offer re-stringing tennis rackets, skates' sharpening and boot fitting - we undertake analysis of both your foot and stride. For trekking and walking boots, we provide a little incline board which you can walk down with on a rough or smooth surface to see whether the toes have enough room in the boots."

The highlight of the shop which is on three floors is the rock climbing wall complete with a bivouac shelter at the top. The wall is used to test boots and initiate children into climbing. Via Ferrata which is a popular activity that can be carried out 30 minutes from Vevey either in Rochers de Naye or Leysin. Translated from the Italian as the iron road, it's a cross between hiking and climbing and Altmann stocks the complete via ferrata kit from Petzl and Mammut which connects you continuously to a safety cable.

"We've also got a range of clothing even for the non-sportive Jaques Tati types from 7 to 77," said François. "There's R'ADY's collection which is extremely light and environmentally friendly as the textiles are free of fluorocarbons. Another fact about R'ADY is that everything is now made in Europe. Among the accessories, I would recommend as essentials are a windbreaker, a space blanket and a gps."

Odile

Rue du Lac 14
Vevey
Tel 079 7189916
info@odile-vintage.com
www.odile-vintage.com

Retro furniture has come into its own. At one time, no one wanted the stuff and it was difficult to sell. Nowadays, it's in great demand and the trend is against antique pieces like Georgian furniture which have lost their value.

Clive Hennessy

Rue du Lac 28
Vevey
Tel 021 921 9345
Mob 0796141576

Clive Hennessy's antique shop in the old town is a place for dreams. All the items in it have a story to tell from the mounted globes with the five continents which can be spun around on their axis to the five-inch thick leather bound ledgers and the miniature toy model of a Chinese cart and two horses. You can imagine Henry James popping in when he stayed round the corner at the Trois Couronnes. His visit would be a welcome break from writing the novel Daisy Miller which was set in Vevey. The walking sticks in an umbrella stand with old polished knobs and handles of precious stones would have instant appeal.

"I can easily imagine the scene," said Clive," because the town still has a feeling of old- world gentility." Then his eyes lit up. "I even have a table from 1870 when Henry James visited the town and wrote the parts which featured Annie. P. Miller, which was Daisy's her real name."

Clive who hails from Cork, Ireland once owned a pub in London and drifted to Switzerland. He followed a woman to Vevey. Later, when she left him, he hesitated to stay at first but decided in the end.

"I started selling bric-a-brac in the market on Tuesday and Saturday," he said with a genial smile. "Then when I found the shop, I went into antiques. Nowadays the market has changed and there's also an interest in retro furniture. So I have a mixture. The huge industrial lamp from the 1980s has the same value as the genuine antique table from the 1870s. They both is cost - CHF 800."

Clive likes meeting people and Vevey always attracted an interesting bunch. There was Sir Hugh Leggatt who bought paintings for the National gallery and lived

Clive Hennessy

Dr Maggiorino Genta, Dr Flavia Genta-Günther who now live in former Cuenod-Churchill bank. Pictured in the strongroom.

round the corner. They met in his shop and he asked Clive for a restaurant and was recommended the Mazot next door. Besides the bohemians who lived in the Chateau de l'Aile on the Place du Marché there was an interesting painter, Danielle-Esmé Cuenod, a descendant the Cuenod-Churchills who entertained many famous artists in her studio including Braque. Clive still has some of her nude sketches in stock.

"I hear all sorts of things from people who cross my threshold," he said. " Hugues-Adhémar Cuénod, the eminent Swiss singer from Corseaux was also related to the Churchills. It was through an illegitimate daughter of the 6th Duke of Marlborough, Susan Harriet Elizabeth Churchill. She was actually the daughter of the Duchess and a relation of the Duke and was taken in by William (later Lord Melbourne) and his wife Lady Caroline Lamb. Susan who was born amid grief, gossip and mystery became a delightful person and later was sent to Switzerland under the care of one of Lord Melbourne's ex-mistresses, Lady Brandon. She found happiness with a curate Aimé Timotheé Cuenod. They married and changed their name to Cuenod-Churchill. Lord Melbourne provided a dowry of £500 and in gratitude, Susan named her children William and Caroline. The couple later founded the Cuenod-Churchill bank in Vevey in 1840."

Clive who has lived in Vevey for over 35 years has like most other inhabitants had sightings of Charlie Chaplin. But as he had never met him he asked the actor's former secretary for an anecdote. "Once when Prime Minister Harold Wilson was invited to lunch," she said, "Charlie could not be found. It was an embarrassing situation as all the guests except the host were seated at the table. I found him at the pool having a drink with the builders. 'Let him wait,' said Chaplin when I requested his presence at the luncheon.'"

"One evening several years after Charlie Chaplin's death," said Clive, "I found myself at a dinner given by Oona Chaplin at their home, Manoir de Ban in Corsier. It was like a dream because I sat next to a chap in a suit whose father had been a docker in London. I thought he was an administrator of the Chaplin family but found out that he was David Bowie. In fact, I later discovered that James Mason had asked Oona to meet Bowie and that was the reason for the dinner. The talk around the table was 'how is John?' (John Lennon). Have you seen Warren lately?(Warren Beatty)."

The next day was market day and Clive was up at 6 am. Later, he saw Oona arrive with the chauffeur to visit the market. She didn't see him but he was happy because he was back to his normal life dealing with ordinary people. He is equally at ease with people from all walks of life. Once there was an old lady who always wore a scarf and bought second hand books from him. They chatted and one day she asked him to look after her handbag.

In her absence another woman popped in and told him it was Greta Garbo. He never saw movie star again.

" My passion is my antiques which keeps me going," he said. "I fell in love with the beauty of the lake at Vevey and I am glad that it will remain the same. People build everywhere today but you can't build on the lake."

Obrist

Avenue Reller 26 CH-1800
Tel 021 9259925
obrist@obrist.ch
www.obrist.ch

Obrist is a Vevey winery which was founded in 1854 by Emmanuel Obrist. It has the best selections of wines in the Montreux Riviera with 600 vintages. The range which is available in their shop, Obrist Vinaria, covers Switzerland, France, Austria, Italy, Spain and the New World - USA, Chile, Argentina and Australia. Pride of place is given to vintages from their own prestigious domaines in the Lavaux and Chablais area. The premier grand cru Château de Chardonne (2013) - chosen through a blind tasting to be the wine of honour for the parliament of Canton Vaud. The other top grand crus are the iconic Clos du Rocher and the Cure d'Attalens, both Chasselas which are very popular and typical of the area.

"We own 55 hectares of vineyards," said Alain Leder, director, "stretching from the terraced vineyards of Lavaux to central Valais with Chablais vineyards halfway between the two. Our goal is optimum quality all the way from the low yield vineyards to contracting out our vines to members of the "Confrérie des Vignerons". These grower-producers follow strict production quality standards that respect cultivation for each variety and terroir."

Wines from Obrist's own production constitute about 65% of the sales and include the original renowned vineyards from the 19th century - La Cure d'Attalens overlooking Vevey and Le Clos du Rocher in Yvorne. Vinification is conducted at the

Obrist winery

1909 headquarters' cellar which contains massive wood barrels, each holding up to 15,000 litres.

Alain Leder who comes from Morges is a high-flyer with an MBA from the university of Lausanne. His background is hospitality and he has had experience in both small hotels and restaurants as well as global companies like Nestlé and Nespresso.

"I'm fortunate as I have worked abroad and experienced different cultures," he said. "On a recent trip to Tokyo with the Office of Vaudois Wine (OVV) to promote our wines, I was surprised by a speech made by a well-known Japanese journalist. He began with the words that Chasselas is 'nothing.' Frankly, I was a bit worried

about the continuation of his speech, but then he qualified his statement with the fact that the variety is discrete, elegant and is a good accompaniment with Japanese cuisine. It doesn't overpower the food but highlights it, and that's true with a lot of different cuisines.

"Travel has made me open-minded. I've learnt to be flexible and to deal with all sorts of situations. I'm always trying to see things with a new eye or at a different angle. It gives me ideas and avoids to get stuck with false certainties. You can't stand still in business, if you don't move forward you go backward."

The trend today in wine is for consumers to go for quality rather than quantity mostly because of changes in consumption

habits and the strict driving laws.
Therefore, Obrist Vinaria stocks top quality vintages such as the 1st Cru Classe Chateau Lafite Rothschild and Chateau Margaux and the Inglenook Estate in Napa Valley. But you will also find a large variety of other top quality wines at all prices.
Obrist is fortunate as it is owned by the Schenk family who pride themselves in acquiring grand domaines and allowing them to continue their traditions. Their ancestor Charles Schenk built the world's largest cask of 23,500 litres for the 1896 Swiss National exhibition in Geneva.
His son, Arnold, who was a vintner, was a visionary who expanded into wineries and domaines across Europe from the headquarters in Rolle.

"Our philosophy is to maintain our commitment to producing quality wine, " François Schenk, "by investing consistently in sustainable vineyards and state of the art technology for winemaking, bottling and storing."

Call me Edouard
Book publisher

Chemin de la Donnaz 1
1802 Corseaux
pm@call-me-edouard
www.call-me-edouard

Call me Edouard is one of the smallest publishers in Switzerland. If it produces two books a year, that's a good average. So far the booklist consists of Graham Greene -The Swiss Chapter by Pierre Smolik which covers the last years of the famous author; Facades and Colors by Nicole Beuchat and Che Huber, a handbook of the colours of the spectrum; and catalogues for the museum Villa "Le Lac" Le Corbusier which include two prominent photographers and a little known but fascinating architect, Alberto Sartoris. If there is a book which epitomises the fine work - both editorial and design, then it is this volume.

The publisher is Patrick Moser whom readers have already met under another guise as a curator of Le Corbusier's Villa "Le Lac." (See entry).

"The story about the name Call me Edouard is extraordinary," said Patrick." It's derived from a fellow inhabitant of Corseaux, Edouard Zahnd, who drove a blue 1930 Bugatti - that looked like a cigar with wheels, and charmed younger women. The old codger tried his chat-up line "just call me Edouard" on my girlfriend, Nicole Beuchat, and it worked. She later suggested that I use the phrase as a name for my publishing house. And then I found an old photograph of men browsing for books after the library at the 17th century Holland House was partly destroyed during the London blitz in 1940. There was a figure dressed in a coat and hat who matched my idea of the logo."

Patrick, the publisher extraordinaire, has the last word. It's about coincidences or what Jung called "synchronicities"

"Edouard Zahnd unveiled the plaque commemorating the 20th anniversary of Graham Greene's death at the Corseaux cemetery," he said. "Then at his funeral

2

four months later, I was standing around the open grave when Graham Greene's daughter, Caroline Bourget, took me by the arm and said, 'You have to help me carry something very heavy.' It turned out to be a watering can filled with water. While burying Edouard, I was watering pansies on Graham Greene's grave. Incredible!"'

Vevey Freeport/Port Franc

Avenue Reller 1
Tel 021 925 3783
sev.vevey@sevpf.ch
www.sevpf.ch

The freeport is the smart way of storing valuable goods such as precious metals, fine art, fine wine, car collections, etc. It is a special customs area where goods can be kept in safe storage without paying any duty or VAT. The facility is a boon to international business as any items can be imported tax-free and only when they are sold is any payment required.

"The freeport storage is of great benefit to art collectors," said Pierre-Alain Perroud, Managing Director of Vevey Port Franc. "We have a client who has homes all over the world including our region. He keeps his artworks in a private area and whenever he's here, he spends hours looking at them. That's his pleasure."

The facility has 4,000 m2 of storage space and goods can be kept on a temporary or permanent basis. The fees are competitive compared to larger freeports such as in Geneva or Luxembourg.

"Our freeport is a Alibaba's Cave as it's filled with all sorts of goods," said Mr Perroud. "It's safe and secure and just a declaration needs to be made about the contents. All that is necessary is to pay the fees for storage."

The other advantages of the freeport is that they provide transport from airports - Geneva is an hour away, and also assist with documentation, insurance, stock management and distribution.

Hotels and restaurants

Hostellerie du Genéve

Place du Marché 11
Tel 021 921 45 77
info@hotelgeneve.ch
www.hotelgeneve.ch

The establishment is run by Anne-Christine Meylan who is the elegant owner. (See entry in People). It's an institution in Vevey and is unmissable - 'à ne pas manquer.' The Hostellerie du Genéve a cafe, a bar, a restaurant and a hotel and is the epitome of the Veveyian soul. It is located in the centre of Vevey, directly on the Place du Marché and just 120 metres from Lake Geneva, featuring an outdoor terrace and free WiFi.

The specialities in the restaurant are veal kidneys with morels, steak tartare alla grappa, steak tagliata with arugula and balsamic vinegar, perch fillets and meat on the grill outdoors or in the restaurant's fireplace in winter.

There is a choice of sections in the restaurant. Besides the main area, La Cantina and the Watchmaker's table provide cosy ambiance for groups or individual guests.

The buffet breakfasts are substantial with baguettes, ham, cheese, quiche, cake, various yoghurts and a range of jams which are also on sale in the boutique.

The 23 rooms are unique and each has a special theme. It depends upon the mood.

2

Anne-Christine Meylan

For example, you can visit countries like China, Morocco and Africa or travel on the Orient Express or on the classic DC-4 aircraft which is a superior double and a 'must' for aviation enthusiasts. It not only has a collection of memorabilia in the room but a metal wingtip serves as a desktop. On the other hand, you might be arty and then you could stay in the Art Deco or contemporary design room. The decor even caters for the Romantic or seasonal like the Autumnal or the Red hot summer. And if your are into the Shades of Grey, there is the Grey room.

Hotel du Léman

Conference Centre
Chemin de la Fontaine
2 Case postale 50
1805 Jongny
Tel 021 923 0303
hotel-leman@coop.ch
www.hotel-leman.ch

The hotel which is situated in a picturesque park in the wine growing village of Jongny is dedicated to seminars, conferences and staff training. What is exceptional about the place is that you can listen, learn and exercise in the open air and every time you look at the surroundings, you automatically want to reach for your camera.

"There's a fundamental value in all of us about nature," said Matthieu Naef, director, "that disarms us when you see such spectacular views. So we have opted for simplicity at the hotel. We're not a mix of spa, gourmet restaurant, beauty salon etc. but specialise in what we do best - seminars. We offer cutting edge technology and are there to support our clients to have a successful event."

The hotel has 64 rooms which is split between the main building and the Villa Praz Verdan which is on a higher level. There are 15 different sized rooms for meetings that can accommodate between 10 and 100 people. They are flexible in terms of room hire - a half or a full day and at times, eight to nine groups can be using the facilities. Between sessions delegates can use the free mountain bikes along the vineyard trails or play table tennis, chess or bowls. The restaurant offers a variety of seasonal menus in the dining areas.

"We are a discreet property with a big heart," he said, "even though we don't have stars, we are positioned as a 3-star superior hotel and have put a big emphasis on customer service and attention to detail. Stars nowadays have lost significance and their real value. You can have all the elements of an upscale luxury hotel but the service can be inconsistent. This is why I have excelled in providing a good and friendly service in all areas. Once a year we have team-building excursion for the staff and it imbues every member with the concept of service."

The hotel follows in the tradition of a training centre which was established 85 year ago by the Coop Group which still owns it. Indeed some 20% of the guests are from all areas of the Group and it's part of the HR division.

Hotel du Léman

Matthieu Naef who lives with his wife, Daniela, and family in St Legier. Daniela is an experienced yoga teacher who is at the centrekaizen.ch in Corseaux. Matthieu studied at the Lausanne Hospitality School and has varied experience in hotels including 5-star brands such as the Four Seasons, Swissotel and the Gstaad Palace. He has a passion for hospitality and is pleased to serve others. It would not be too complimentary to mention that he is one of the friendliest hotelier in the region. But the message is also becoming known to tourists who are impressed by the comfort and wellbeing in dreamlike surroundings.

Trois Couronnes hotel

Rue d'Italie 49
1800 Vevey
Tel 021 923 3200
infohoteltroiscouronnes.ch
www.hoteltroiscouronnes.ch

The award-winning hotel is built on the foundations of an old Swiss castle (the vaults of which can still be seen at the spa), and is set against the timeless backdrop of Lake Geneva and the beautiful Alps. Known as a legendary artists' hideaway on the Swiss Riviera, it offers 71 individually decorated rooms, of which 16 suites and 9 junior suites. Its Puressens Destination Spa features several health and treatment programmes and a 24m indoor swimming pool with underwater music. Tailored treatments from world-renowned skin specialist Joëlle Ciocco (exclusivity for Switzerland) are available.

The 1-star Michelin restaurant, Les Trois Couronnes, offers gourmet cuisine with excellent local seasonal food products. The newly designed restaurant, The Lounge, is the place to enjoy a more casual cuisine in a trendy and informal way.

Jay Gauer who is the General Manager of the Trois Couronnes hotel in Vevey is a gifted hotelier. He knows that to market his hotel successfully it is important to sell the destination.

"Vevey is situated within an hour radius of what is considered to be a miniature Switzerland," he said with passion. "Visitors can experience the essential elements of Swissness - chocolates, cheese, wines, gastronomy, culture, and watchmaking. Within 20 minutes, they can visit a cheese factory close to the historic village of Gruyères and the Cailler-Nestle

chocolate factory in Broc. There's even a chocolate train that is laid on for tourists from May to October and includes a cheese dairy. Within one hour you can be in the watchmaking area of Jura."

Vevey, the city where milk chocolate was invented in 1875, has great attractions and experiences. A highlight is the Festival Images which is the largest monumental photography festival in the world and transforms the city into an open sky museum. Special packages arranged by the hotel's concierge will enable guests to learn how to assemble a watch. Every Wednesday and Saturday, the traditional market takes place on the Place du Marché, one of the largest market squares in Europe.

"Switzerland is a beautiful destination," he said. "What counts more for a destination is the emotional appeal. The most important when you travel is the one-of-a-kind stories you will bring home with you. If, instead of just buying some chocolate in Switzerland, you can actually learn how make your own chocolate, this is story you will keep forever. Another example is the molecular cuisine demonstration by award winning Chef Denis Martin in his R&D laboratory, where one can for example learn how to cook pasta without water. There's also an exciting opportunity of eating in the kitchen of 3-star Michelin restaurant. Benoît Violier, considered to be one of the world's 15 best chefs, offers such an experience. An important part of our job is creating or selecting such added value experiences for our guests."

Jay Gauer is a third generation hotelier. He grew up in Bern where his father ran the Schweizerhof hotel. His first experience of hotel work was at the age of 8. He graduated with a Business Administration degree at Geneva and spent a year with a private equity company which invested in hotels, restaurants and casinos. Then his career changed radically from spread sheets to hotel operations and later he assumed a position of General Manager at the Hôtel des Trois Couronnes.

Without doubt Jay Gauer is a veritable ambassador for the Swiss Riviera and the neighbouring towns. His enthusiasm is a great plus for the city of Vevey and the hotel Trois Couronnes. It inspires tourists to visit and to enjoy the best attractions.

Le Mirador Kempinski

Chemin de l'hotel du Mirador 5
1801 Le Mont-Pèlerin
Tel 021 9251111
reservations.lemirador@kempinski.com
www.kempinski.com/mirador

"It's a Wow location. I felt the same years ago when I first passed through Montreux. Real luxury is peace. That's what you find here. In my definition, there are two types of luxury: standard and s pecial. It's like an artpiece and a masterpiece respectively. The masterpiece takes great talent, time and patience. This is what we have at the Mirador Kempinski." Jean-Marc Boutilly who runs the five-star family hotel with his wife.

The Mirador has 61 bedrooms including nine suites and 47 junior suites. It has a Givenchy Spa, medical centre, swimming pool, fitness centre and three restaurants with Europe's most spectacular terrace. It has a helipad and is used by guests who can't wait to return to the peaceful ambiance and top of the world view.

Anyone who comes to the Montreux Riviera should not miss the Mirador Kempinski. The breakfast alone with the juicer to make your own vegetable drink, the slab of butter - no little pots will suffice and the wide range of seasonal fare makes it one of the best in the region.

Astra Hotel Vevey

Place de la Gare 4
Vevey
www.astra-hotel.ch
Tel 021 925 04 04

Astra Hotel Vevey is a world class hotel in the centre of Vevey. Surprised? You shouldn't be because Christophe Ming who manages it with his brother Nicolas trained at two famous luxury establishments - the Beau Rivage Palace in Lausanne-Ouchy and the Brown Palace in Denver, Colorado. The brothers are the third generation to run the 4-star superior hotel with 100 rooms and suites, a conference centre for 200 and 24-hour business centre. Special features include an atrium lobby, a rooftop terrace with a jacuzzi and the historic brasserie, La Coupole 1912 with exclusive paintings and stained glass windows of the Winegrowers Festivals.

"Our location is unique because we're right in the centre of Vevey and opposite the train station," said Christophe. "It's so convenient for meetings, conferences and visitors as they just step off the train and in two minutes are inside the hotel. Then they can use the spa facilities to rid themselves of travel fatigue or swing into action in the fitness room."

In 1950, Joseph Ming, the great uncle of the two hoteliers acquired the site and in 1965, their parents Niklaus and Monique Ming took over the management. The byword of the family has been personal service and they try to ensure that each guest is made to feel at home. Christophe who grew up in the hotel never doubted his future career and after serving his apprenticeship at the Beau Rivage Palace widened his experience in the US. The Brown Palace Hotel was just the place as it hosted every American president since the 1890s except Calvin Coolidge. It's a 240-room luxury hotel in Denver Colorado that features six restaurants, a spa and an atrium lobby with live music.

"During my internship in 1997 and 1998, I was fortunate not only to see President Clinton," said Christophe, "but the leaders from Britain, Canada, Japan, Italy, France and Germany who comprised the G-7 at the Denver Library."
A visit or stay at the Astra hotel Vevey would not be complete without dining at the Brasserie La Coupole. Guests can sit in the large brasserie and admire the magnificent stained glass dome and depictions of the three last Winegrower festivals of 1955, 1977 and 1999. The artworks by Michel Delanoë were commissioned by Christophe and Nicolas Ming to commemorate the 100th anniversary of the Brasserie. Copies of the Bieler illustrations for the 1927 Winegrower festival also adorn the walls.

Le Montagne
David Tarnowski

Rue du Village 21
1803 Chardonne
Tel 021 921 2930
le-montagne@bluewin.ch
www.le-montagne.com

Le Montagne is the restaurant that has got it all. A panoramic view, a terrace, a classy decor, accolades from Michelin and Gault Millau and great food. David Tarnowski who has the makings of a top chef, learnt early on in his career to do it the right way. No short-cuts.

"I worked with one of the giants of gastronomy, Paul Ducasse," he said, "and obtained a thorough understanding French contemporary haute cuisine through him. Later it was through him that I got a position of chef at the new restaurant at the Fairmont Montreux Palace. Within 15 months we had got a Michelin star and Gault Millau."

There are three signature dishes at the restaurant. The starter Foie gras du sud with en fine royal, tawny port, granny smith and old vinegar is one of them and he sets the tone with complex and delicate flavours. The tastes are intriguing and one is silent for a second because its unexpected on the palate but works perfectly in combination. The dish is served warm to stimulate the tastebuds.

Laurence and David Tarnowski

Another is a main course which features a fine purée (mousseline) of sea bass with juice and leaves of artichoke and mashed potatoes. But it is also the artistic arrangement on the plate that catches the eye. If salt is used it is a question of tasting several grains and not salty dish. The dessert was a visual surprise as it was served in a large wine glass which was tilted to show its contents. The name of Coupelle bellevue is justified because you can see the view through it. It is a mixture of tastes of kakis and mango, paste of saffron as well as mango sorbet and ginger. "I was introduced to my future career on my aunt's farm," said Tarnowski. "She kept a variety of animals such as cows, goats, sheep and poultry and even rabbits. I helped with the milking of cows and haymaking. It was there that I learnt about

Dessert Coupelle Bellevue

eating raw vegetables like carrots and turnips. There is a distinctive taste between the two. Today, I believe that taste is the most important element in cooking besides the quality."

Tarnowski was born in Venissieux outside Lyon and studied at the local school of hospitality. Like most top chefs he knew at an early age that he wanted a career in cooking. It was not an easy path and he was prepared to travel to Tulsa, Oklahoma for his first job. But he was determined to succeed and soon began his ascent into the Michelin starred establishments like the Hotel Martinez in Cannes under Christian Willer and La Terrace restaurant at Hotel Juana in Antibes under Christian Morisset.

But his imprimatur is not only on the food, it extends to the decor of the restaurant. There is a sense of the dramatic because the curtains which are an orange-brown hang like huge ties with knots at the top, the ball-like flower arrangements on plinths and the natural sculpture - an incredible skeleton of a plane tree complete with its root formation. On Mothers' and Valentine Day the decor changes to plum and purple.

"I'm also like combining the old with the new," he said, "for example with the crockery used in the restaurant. It's another form of visual delight to see the different shapes and colours.

I've even found a practical solution with the modern cheese trolley which when not in use is stored in a customised wooden cupboard that conceals the smell."

There is little doubt that David Tarnowski who loves the Montreux Riviera will bring glory to the region through his creative contemporary haute cuisine. He is proud of his wife, Laurence, whom he describes as his best employee and his two children. Although, he knows that restaurant = 3 x work, he is determined to also find time for his family.

Charly's

Rue du Lac 45
Vevey
Tel 021 921 5006

Charly's is full of surprises. On the rue du lac it's a cafe and when you ascend the staircase you find the restaurant with a terrace which is right on the lake with the best view in Vevey. On the lakeside there's also a scotch bar and tables where you can have fish and chips. Or if you prefer you can eat perch from the lake or steak in the upstairs in the enclosed dining room. But wherever, the setting is magnificent. Jacques Oliger who is the owner is also full of surprises. He was an Olympic athlete and was born in Chile where his father was the French consul.

"I spend the winter months every year in Patagonia, southern Chile," he said. "I have a farm on the back of the Andes and the climate is similar to the Montreux Riviera. The farm is 150 km from the nearest town of Valdivia."

Brasserie La Coupole

Astra Hotel Vevey
Place de la Gare 4
Vevey
www.astra-hotel.ch
Tel 021 925 04 04

The restaurant is run by the third generation of the Ming family. They are very Swiss with a great tradition in hospitality which is shown in their attention to detail. The menu ranges from typical brasserie dishes like classic steak frites, beef and fish tartare, sauerkraut

Stained glass dome

Copy of Bieler mural

to Swiss specialities such as roesti and raclette. There is also an international cuisine. The gourmet plat de jour is recommended and the desserts are excellent.

What is outstanding is the brasserie decor which provides it with an authentic ambiance for it was first opened in 1912. The stain glass dome and windows celebrate the unique Winegrower Festivals which are held each generation. The copies of Bieler murals add to the atmosphere.

In all, there are three restaurants at the Astra: the light and airy Pavillon, the Quatre Saisons with its modern decor and the historic Brasserie La Coupole. The cosy Orient Express bar with its regional selection of wines, champagnes, aperitifs and digestives and snack menu which is available until 22.30. An added benefit for guests and clients is the Astra Roof lounge and its terrace with the splendid view of Mont Pèlerin and the Lavaux vineyards.

Auberge de la Veveyse

Route de Châtel-St-Denis 212
1806 St-Legier
Tel 021 943 6760
www.auberge-de-la veveyse.ch

There are Michelin starred restaurants and Michelin starred restaurants. The definition of the star or stars is very good, exceptional or exquisite cuisine worth a journey. Some like the Auberge de la Veveyse go the extra mile for their customers.

Jean-Sébastian Ribette and Sahondra Verdan chose a lovely setting in the countryside rather than in a city because they wanted people to be relaxed when they come to enjoy the cuisine. The yellow and blue building is on the former site of a coaching inn on the road to Bern. There is the choice of the gourmet restaurant or the brasserie which in summer offers a terrace under the shade of a magnificent lime tree.

Events

Brotherhood of Winegrowers Confrérie des Vignerons Museum

Rue du Chateau 2
Vevey
Tel 021 923 8705
confrerie@fetedesvignerons.ch
www.fetedesvignerons.ch

The most spectacular event in the Montreux Riviera occurs once in about 20 years. It's the Fête des Vignerons (Festival of the Winegrowers) which has been organised by the Confrérie des Vignerons (Brotherhood of Winegrowers) since 1797. Back then in the 18th century, there were 2,000 spectators to watch the parade and at the last festival in 1999, it had risen to over 240,000. What began as a simple procession from St Martin's church to the lake front with the Brotherhood's flag and the statue of St Urban at its head, has become a giant outdoor theatre to celebrate its love of wine.

"I'm the seventh generation to be involved on the board of the Confrérie des Vignerons," said François Margot who is the president of the Festival of the Winegrowers 2019. "Both my grandfather and father have also been involved on the board and in the former festivals. The organising committee is free to choose how often the festival takes place but the maximum number is five times a century. The interval between them has varied from 14 to 28 years. The interval between the last and the next is 20 years."

The oldest document possessed by the society were minutes which were given to the Brotherhood by the wise, prudent and virtuous Lord abbot of agriculture of Vevey under the patronage of Saint Urban of Langres on June 22, 1647. The society has a Benedictine motto, Ora et Labora (pray and work) and is headed by the Abbot-president. A prized possession is the wooden Abbot's cup with medallions round the top of the names of successive Abbots. Inside the cup is the name Gaspar Rot 1618.

The membership grew during the 18th century and by 1776, almost 25% of the male population belonged to the society. At first the parade through town was followed by a general meeting and a banquet. In 1797, when fetes became fashionable, the first stands were built in the market square to accommodate people attending the crowning of the best vineyard worker.

"It's important to know that it was not a guild to defend the interests of a profession or a trade," said Margot, "nor is it an association of workers like a trade union but a group of landowners who entrusted the care of the vineyards to vineyard workers. Around 1770, the Brotherhood decided that it's aim was to encourage improvements in grape growing and rewarding the good results of the vineyard workers. The most successful received a crown and an award. Nowadays, they have silver and bronze medals and a total of cash prizes of CHF 100,000. The gold medal is only given at festivals."

The Brotherhood currently inspects 270 hectares of vineyards between Lausanne and Lavey on the border with the Valais. The inspections are undertaken by seven experts who visit three times a year. During the spring, it's to observe pruning and in the summer, to examine vine stocks and anti-parasite measures. While in the autumn, the quality of the soil is noted and the physical appearance and management of the grape harvest.

After each visit, marks are awarded to vineyard workers and sent to the owners and winegrowers. The total marks of each worker results in a ranking after three years and they are awarded prizes at a ceremony called the Triennale. However, during the festival which is a momentous event in a generation, the workers are judged over three to five previous years. The event serves as a grand platform for the prizewinners.

"In June 2011, it was announced by the council of the Brotherhood that the next festival would be in 2019," said Margot. "It took another two years to select the creative director of the festival. The candidates came from a wide field including theatre, arts, music, journalism and communications. In the end, we chose Daniele Finzi Pasça who comes from Ticino. His vision and values closely resembled the Brotherhood's concept of the 2019 festival."

In 1851, François Grast composed the first complete score that gave a certain unity to the lyrics which were a mixture of texts written by various amateur poets. He also wrote the score for the 1865 Festival. In 1905, a complete work was finally achieved, thanks to the close collaboration of the Morax brothers, René and Jean, respectively librettist and painter, with the composer Gustave Doret. They created a veritable hymn to nature and the land, and its success affected generations of singers. Preparations by the participants for the 2019 festival will begin about two years before. The costumes have to be designed and created, the dances choreographed, the music written, choirs have to practice, the grandstand and scenery has to be constructed.

"Can you imagine that almost 5,000 actors and almost 4,000 dancers are involved?" said Margot. "And 20-25% of those are children under 16. We start building the huge arena in February 2019. Traffic can no longer pass through the market square. The amateur singers, dancers and actors take their annual holidays three weeks before the event which will run for about two and a half weeks, from July 26th to August 11. There'll be two or three parades from Vevey to La Tour de Peilz. And it's been going on since 1791! And we still have the flag from the first parade which depicts Bacchus as a child seated on a wine barrel."

Chapter 3. Lavaux Vineyards

History

There are two views of the Lavaux vineyards. Just look across the lake to France and you will see what it was like a 1,000 years ago. Nature dominates the slopes and hills with forests except for several settlements on the lakeshore. On the Swiss side, it's radically changed. The hand of man is apparent as the landscape is covered by thousands of terraces and hundreds of kilometres of walls. In addition, the architecture of the narrow houses of the winemakers bunched together in 14 villages contrast with the prominent buildings of the large estates. At one end of Lavaux, you have Lutry with the hamlets Châtelard and Savuit, and in the heart of the vineyards is Cully with Grandvaux, Riex, Villette and Epesses, then Rivaz, Chexbres and St Saphorin and finally Chardonne, Corseaux and Vevey. A unique cultural landscape which was designated a UNESCO World Heritage Site in June 2007.

The Lavaux vineyards which stretch over 30 km from Lausanne to Montreux are one of the most impressive sights in the world. Steep slopes rise high above the blue waters of lake Geneva and offer spectacular panoramic views. The terraced landscape with its stone walls is also known as the Land of the Three Suns. The sun from the sky, from the lake which acts as a mirror and from the walls which absorb heat.

The landscape of steep hills with slopes from 15% to 100% were formed by the glacial period in 13,000 BC. Consequently, the soil consists of a mass of rocks and sediment carried and deposited by the glacier with a varied content of clay, limestone and a variety of minerals.

From the 12th century several monasteries were established on land given by the Bishop of Lausanne to the Cistercians and Benedictines. The monks cleared the hillsides and planted grapevines. They built terraces and contained them with walls to prevent erosion. By the 14th century, the vineyards had expanded and the monks were encouraged to lease land to tenants in return for a percentage of their crops. Terraces allotted were 10 -15 m wide and were supported by walls of 5 to 6 m high. The tenants were also required to maintain the walls and 'slides' for water run-offs. Many of the winemakers like Chappuis, Duboux, Fonjallaz and de

Mestral are direct descendants who have tended to the vineyards for more than 17 generations. This cultural landscape of Lavaux constitutes Switzerland largest vineyards and displays evolution and development over 1,000 years.

The criteria to be listed as a UNESCO World Heritage Site was based on the exceptional witness to a cultural tradition, an outstanding example of interaction between people and their environment over centuries and illustrated graphically the control, patronage and protection of a highly valued wine region.

The Lavaux Patrimoine mondial (LPm) is an association tasked with the guardianship of the vineyards. Its aim is to protect and to enhance the values of Lavaux with four guidelines: Economy and viticulture, land planning, communication and culture, education and tourism. Jean-Jacques Gauer who is the director of the Lausanne Palace hotel is the president. The website is www.lavaux-unesco.ch

The Lavaux from an oenological perspective covers four main districts - Dezelay, Calamin, Epesses and St Saphorin as well as eight soil profiles. The districts have multiple personalities. Dezelay has three distinct terroirs and different climates. The grapes in the high and cold part of Dezelay are harvested 10 to 14 days later than in the lakeside of Cully. Dezelay and Calamin are the only ones that are Grand Cru. The slopes of Dezelay are the steepest in the Lavaux because the rock lying beneath it is so hard that it did not yield to the four glaciers that gouged out the lake and sculpted the shore.

Chasselas is a good match for this geological quilt because it is a chameleon, readily absorbing the character of its particular terroir. The wine lacks strong aromatics and is not often improved by manipulation in the winery such as malolactic fermentation or oak ageing.

"Sometimes, what you making is an oak ageing juice," said Jerome Ake, sommelier and Manager of the auberge de l'Onde.

When you drink Chasselas, in a way you are drinking the soil. The stone foundations of Dezelay produce wines with a pronounced mineral or even flinty character whereas the gravel and chalk of St Saphorin yields a slightly viscous and aperitif quality wine. Lower down in Calamin which lies just above the lake, the grape has a thicker texture and bitter finish as a result of 30% limestone over very thick clay.

"It's called terroir roulez which reflects the fact that it rolled down and came to rest here," said Blaise Duboux, a winegrower from Epesses whose descendants are traced to the 15th century.

Louis-Philippe Bovard who is from Cully is the doyen of the winemakers in the Lavaux vineyards. He is the 10th generation to run his family's 16 hectare estate and he started making wine to go with food rather than as an aperitif. Ahead of the game, he introduced new varieties like Sauvignon Blanc (his Buxus), oak-aged Chasselas, stopped using fertilizer because he thought it diminished the acidity and created a conservatory of 19 varieties of Chasselas. His Grand Cru Calamin Chasselas Ilex is vinified in wood with no malolactic fermentation. He also has Grand Cru whites and three reds from Dezaley which is considered to be the best domaine.

Chexbres

Pierre-Luc Leyvraz

Chemin de Baulet 4
1071 Chexbres
Tel 021 946 1940
www.leyvraz-vins.ch

He is one of the smallest winemakers in Lavaux with about 3.5 hectares. He's a one-man band for he prunes, picks with three seasonal workers, checks the grapes at the collecting point, ferments them and does the accounting at night. He wins awards and the St- Saphorin Grand Cru Les Blessings is one of his best.

Lucien Moutarlier

Grand Rue
1071 Chexbres
Tel 021 946 1815
www.moutarlier.ch,

Branches in Lutry, Mountreux

Lucien Moutarlier who was born in Nantes, France now lives with his family in Chexbres. He is a patisseur, confiseur and traiteur with shops in Lutry, Lausanne, Chexbres and Montreux. His two sons, Damien who is a patisseur and Christophe,

View of Vevey from Chexbres

a chocolatier, work with him.

Le Baron Tavernier

Route de la Corniche
Casa Postale 90
CH-1070 Puidoux/Chexbres
Tel 021 926 6000
www.barontavernier.ch

The Baron Tavernier is a boutique hotel with 22 bedrooms and suites, each with balconies, that have a beautiful panorama on the Alps, Geneva lake and the Lavaux vineyards. But the WOW factor is the view from the Deck which is one of the best in the Montreux Riviera.

A special feature is the wellness and medi-spa with high-tech Technogym equipment. There is also a sauna, a hamam, a saline pool that is warmed professionally to provide super relaxation plus a whirl section that you control at your convenience as well as complimentary tea, nuts and dried fruits. Various massages are offered to rebalance the body, detoxify or for pure pleasure as well as scented beauty treatments from Morocco.

Gaudenz Dorta, the director comes from Scuol Tarasp in the Grisons. He was introduced to hospitality in his boyhood through his grandmother's cooking. It inspired him to begin a career as an apprentice chef at the 5-star Baur au Lac in Zurich.

"She lived on the first floor of the house and her spicy smells wafted upwards," he said. "My favourite dishes still originate from that time like fish curry soup which is served on rice. "

Mr Dorta is proud of the three dining options at the hotel. Le Baron which has an intimate and welcoming decor. The menu consists of an innovative market-fresh cuisine based on classical French foundations. Fish from the lake, lamb from Montreux and seasonal fruit and vegetables. Le Bon Sauvage with its selection of meat, fish, pasta and vegetarian dishes that would delight a passing gourmet. It even has a daily tart selection made by the pastry chef. And then the Deck which is open from April to October and has incredible views over lake Geneva. Its summer menu is inspired by the Mediterranean.

"What I've found over the years, "he said, " is that simple dishes done well are better than complicated things that have no taste."

There is little doubt that a visit to Baron Tavernier which is located in the heart of the Lavaux vineyards at an elevation of some 600m will invigorate the senses. The spectacular view, the mountain air, the sounds of nature, the taste of good food and the massages: all one needs is to experience it!

Art History

In August 1946, Marcel Duchamp, the French American artist and his companion, Mary Reynolds, came to the Montreux Riviera and stayed at the Bellevue hotel in Chexbres. They wrote to their friends, the French Ambassador Henri Hoppenot and his wife Helene of the changing colour every hour of the water in the lake. They were also overcome by the beauty of Vevey.

In a postscript, they informed the Hoppenots that they had contacted Edouard Flouck, an estate agent, who would help in finding them a dream house in the region. On August 22, Mr Flouck showed Duchamp and Reynolds, La Folie 16 de la Route de Chardonne which the Hoppenots subsequently bought. Mr Flouck who had established his agency in 1941 was unaware of the importance of his clients.

St Saphorin

St Saphorin is one of the picturesque villages in the Lavaux vineyards. It has narrow steep cobbled streets and old winemaker's houses crowded round fountains and alleys. It lies along the Roman highway and the little church has a small museum of Roman artefacts. Some 30% of the land is used for vineyards.

Auberge de l'Onde

Centre du village
1071 St Saphorin
Tel 021 925 4900
info@aubergedelonde.ch
www.aubergedelonde.ch

Auberge de l'Onde which is an old inn from the 16th century and once a major stop for stagecoaches plying between Geneva and Italy. Today it is known for the renowned restaurant which is run by an even more renowned restaurateur and sommelier Jerome Ake.

The Auberge de l'Onde is on three levels and offers a grill room, two restaurants and a music lounge. It has re-invented itself during Jerome Ake's stewardship. Indeed, it was known for its grilled chicken and meat and was a meeting place for various locals and artists whose ink portraits by Gea Augsbourg don the walls in the brasserie on the ground floor. Jean-Villard-Gilles, a Swiss songwriter and poet was a habitué.

"When I came here, the restaurant had a Michelin star," he said. "It also had all the accoutrements that go with it - the chichiness of the staff, the small helpings on the plate. But you tended to forget the guests and think about the star. We thought that was a mistake and changed the emphasis. Our main aim now is to

St Saphorin

St Saphorin

provide a good atmosphere, good food, make the guests feel at home so that they would come back. We lost the star but it was worth it."

Who would have thought that someone from Africa, from the Ivory coast a country with no wine, could become a wine expert extraordinaire. And to continue the remarkable story, he became the maître d'hôtel and sommelier of the legendary inn, l'Onde, St-Saphorin. Jerome Ake who lives in Vevey with his family, is the person who achieved such an amazing career.

"I studied catering in Abidjan and came to Switzerland to improve my knowledge in 1990," he said. "As I am French-speaking, I started to work in the Montreux Riviera at the best restaurants like Auberge du Raisin, L'Ermitage and Denis Martin at Le Chateau, Vevey. Then by accident, I was launched into the world of sommeliers.

"At the time, I was at the Trianon restaurant, Mirador Kempinski under Eric Favre and the management were determined to win a Michelin star. So we got all geared up and got our Michelin star. In 2003, we hosted the Champagne Ruinart Sommelier Award and at the last moment, we didn't have a sommelier. The General Manager asked me to step into the breach three months before and I'm like a zero. No knowledge, nothing. But I accepted the challenge on one condition. I needed an extra day off a week to prepare which he gave me."
The House of Ruinart which is one of the oldest champagne houses, was founded by Nicolas Ruinart in 1729. The Ruinart trophy for the Best Sommelier in France was created in 1979. It was followed in 1988 for the best Sommelier in Europe and in 2004 for the best Sommelier in the Americas.

"I ended up finishing in the top three," he said in his amiable manner. "That was the first time they saw a black man. The results were headlined in a newspaper: a woman, a white and a black. Today, if I'm asked what makes a good sommelier, I would answer: a good memory and listen to the guest. I compare it to a DJ who doesn't just play what he likes but what his audience likes too."

Jerome Ake has been restaurant manager and sommelier of Auberge de l'Onde for over nine years. During that period the auberge had undergone a renovation under its new owner George Muller. He created the gourmand restaurant on the first floor with its modern decor but retained the old fireplace with its mechanical revolving spit. Mr Muller who bought the restaurant knew it as a child and had proposed to his wife there. The previous owner Patrick Fonjallaz who can trace his descendants to the 16th century has the illustrious guest book which includes Charlie Chaplin and Igor Stravinsky.

"From then on, I began to learn about wine," he said, "and if I do something, I do it seriously. There's a system for learning about wine. The structure of the vintage, colour, nose and mouth - the first taste, the middle taste and the aftertaste. But most important of all is the memory. You must

Jerome Ake ©Edouard Curchod

be able to recognise the taste forever. The best way to learn about wine is to visit the winemaker not in books. The first thing you learn is about the terroir or soil. You can smell it in the wine. Take the example of the white wine made from Chasselas grapes grown in the vineyard just behind the church. There's a strong minerality and a particular flavour we call pierre à fusil or gunpowder. It's the smell of two rocks being scraped together. It's that taste, that smell which is prized in wines from Lavaux."

"I'm passionate about wine," he said. "When its paired with food, you must get a good fusion. Both must go in the same direction. You don't want one to dominate the other. Keep the best wine like a Margaux to drink with the main meal. I'm not a stickler about the custom of drinking red wine with meat and white wine with fish. For example, I recommend that a steak tartare be drunk with a white wine like a Chasselas because the tannin of a red can kill the taste of finest meat. In general a white wine like Chasselas can go with everything."

There is another side to Jerome Ake. He not only has a nose for wine but for perfume. He blends his own aromas. It was in a perfume shop in Vevey that he met his future wife called Sara. She is Swiss and was born in Aigle.

Life has been a challenge for Jerome Ake who has become one of the top sommeliers in Switzerland. It's not bad for someone who was used only to imbibing pineapple juice in his youth. He found that he has a sharp palate for Lavaux wines and is an expert on Chasselas. The very best are made in the Dezaley area from the towns of Epesses and Villette to Chardonne. He lives by the simple maxim. "Don't be afraid of challenge because life is a challenge. If there was no challenge, there would be no hope."

Jerome Ake has written two books - The best 50 winemakers in Switzerland and the 99 Chasselas you should drink before you die. He is also the only sommelier who is a member of the Association of the Swiss Memory and the Compagnon Jurie. He scored a first in Switzerland through the production of L'Onde Noir which is a blend of Vaud and Valais Syrah wines. Unthinkable because Cantons don't like to mix their wines.

Kilo Art

Pierre Keller who was born in the vineyards of the village Gilly near Rolle not far from Chateau Vincy where both Voltaire and Alphonse de Lamartine stayed. He now lives in St Saphorin. His philosophy of life is to wake up early in the morning even if you went to bed late. To work hard and be an optimist. But above all, never take yourself seriously but to do everything seriously.

His life is a tour de force. He is an artist in graphic and plastic arts, an events organizer, a publisher, a teacher, an art consultant, an exhibition curator and art collector. He represented Switzerland in the International Poster Biennale, Warsaw; the Ninth Biennale des Jeunes, Paris; the 17th International Biennal, São Paolo and represented Vaud Canton at the 700th anniversary of the Swiss Confederation. He is a member of the Foundation Board of the Montreux Jazz Festival and Professor of EPFL (the Federal Institute of Technology), Lausanne. But his most outstanding and lasting achievement is as the director of Lausanne University of Art and Design or Ecole Cantonale d'Art de Lausanne (ECAL). Concurrently, he is known as the master in Swiss graphic design and without doubt an 'passeur extraordinaire of ideas.' In the UK, he would have been showered with honours like a knighthood and called Sir Pierre Keller or even elevated to the House of Lords, Lord Keller.

In 1965, Pierre graduated from "Ecole Cantonale des beaux-arts et d'arts appliqués" in Lausanne with first class honours and started a multifaceted and brilliant career as an artist. To achieve this, he travelled extensively. His quest was to find out how to combine art and industrial design, a subject which had disconcerted a generation of artists, specially those into kinetic art and optics. In Italy, he worked with Eugenio Carmi whose art successfully integrates various aspects of the visual experience. There's no linear path to describe his work for he combines painting, photography, collages, design and visual poetry. But it gave him a head start.

"At 16, I entered the School of Art and Design Lausanne to exit graphic art four years later," said Pierre Keller. "Then I went to Italy, England, Canada and the United States. From these years, I created my network. I got to know great artists like Jean Tinguely, Christo, Keith Haring, Andy Warhol, Gordon Matta-Clark, Robert Mapplethorpe and Nan Goldin. I started my art collection with a Fontana silk screen, a Balthus drawing and a Keith Haring."

Warhol's factory

In 1972, influenced by Marcel Duchamp, he became interested in conceptual art and created Kilo art. It would be the standard of identity and of beauty which was authenticated by the Swiss Federal Patent office. During the mid 1970s, he began to use photography, specially the Polaroid camera as his artistic medium to record his American period. When Keller was in New York, Warhol's factory at 860 Broadway at the north end of Union Square was a hip hang out for artsy types, amphetamine users and the Warhol superstars. Happenings were staged there and included nudity, graphic sexuality, drug use, same-sex relations and transgender characters.

"I met Keith Haring when I began seeing his chalk drawings on black paper in subways," said Pierre. "The first time was at 63rd and Lexington and then at Bloomingdales 1000 Third avenue. We became good friends and I bought a work from him in those early days. I paid $50. In 1983, he made a poster for the Montreux Jazz Festival. Nan Goldin, the American photographer was another friend whose famous work was the Ballad of Sexual Dependency(1986). The snapshots show drug use, violent, aggressive couples and autobiographical

Pierre Keller

moments. Later, most of the people in the book died of drug overdoses or AIDS. I shared with these friends and Andy Warhol the conviction that sexual depiction like Courbet's Origin of the World is also the origin of the photographic images. These damned images examine the lowest level, the emptiness where the human body exhibits himself. This is the ultimate face of creation and pleasure and its violence."

Keller's oeuvre of photos which span 1977 to 1988 are in the book, Pierre Keller, published by JRP/Ringier Kunstverlag (2011). They include two nude self-portraits, Andy Warhol and Keith Haring, Jean Tinguely, examples from his polaroid collection, Haras de Cluny and cities such as New York, Tokyo, Hammamet, Cairo, Bogota and São Paulo, among others.

"The Swiss painter and sculptor, Jean Tinguely, is another friend," said Pierre. "He designed a poster for the Canton Vaud on the 700th anniversary of the Swiss Confederation and made a special tie - we end up selling 60,000. I'm also proud that I have over 100 letters from Tinguely which are beautifully illustrated with collages and text."

In 1995, he was appointed the director of Ecole Cantonale d'Art de Lausanne (ECAL). It was defining moment of his life and he poured everything into ECAL - his experience, know-how and his oversized black diary of contacts. He was given three goals: compete for university status, increase the school's reputation in Switzerland and build its reputation abroad. The first obstacle was the staff because him appointment was not well received by them.

"When I arrived, professors were just teaching not working outside in the field," he said. "You have a professor aged 55 who had a good eye but who hasn't ever worked on a Mac. I quickly set out to reinvigorate my teaching staff and the average age became 33. I also wined and dined stars like Ronan Bouroullec when they were still relatively unknown. They were invited to come and teach while they had space to work on personal projects."

Zhejiang Art Museum

"Education has to be flexible, fast and interdisciplinary," he said. "It has to be different from what it was 20 years ago. This is not a school of learning. Our students are measured by what is being done best in their field. We put them in touch with and network with the real world of industry, art and creation. The rebellious artist in his attic has been finished for a long time. What interests me is to have young creators, whether graphic designers, typographers or artists who feed the visual culture today. Young designers quickly understand and anticipate things, they are image-makers who do not see the same as the rest of the world. They discover and convey the world in a particular way. Their input can affect both the visual identity of a company, a new typography, a tool or functional design."

Part of Keller's brief was to secure sponsorship and funding to get them working with a selection of the world's creative companies. One of the first sponsorships he obtained was from the founder of IKEA, Ingvar Kamprad, who donated CHF 300,000 for IKEA's auditorium. He also auctioned off the naming right of the 350 seats in the building for CHF 500 each. His fundraising involved extensive travel for about 40 weeks of the year. One of the novel courses he introduced was a master in advanced studies that resulted in design for luxury and craftsmanship and enabled students to work in top luxury brands in the world.

"It's like a private company," he said, "my clients are my students and I do my best for my clients. Without them I would close. While some higher education institutions stress theory over industry contacts, I'm keen to emphasise results. I don't think about methodology, I think about the students."

ECAL is located on the outskirts of Lausanne in what was an abandoned hosiery factory which architect, Bernard Tschumi, transformed into a high-tech education facility decorated in primary colours with an undulating metal facade. When Keller's tenure ended in 2011, ECAL was not only competing with London's Royal College of Art and Eindhoven's Design Academy but was one of the top ten leading design schools in the world.

Pierre Keller has won accolades from different quarters. "Design schools are the most important centres for the production of ideas," said Paola Antonelli, senior curator in the department of architecture and design, Museum of Modern Art (MOMA), New York. She describes Keller as a "tornado of ideas, an irresistible force in the world of design."

Another tribute comes from a friend, Jean-Claude Biver, a pioneer of Swiss watchmaking and head of LVMH's watch brands. "Pierre Keller embodies what Switzerland stands for today," he said "a Switzerland out to conquer the future but with its roots still firmly planted in the soil and in the strength of the past."

Pierre Keller has received various awards. Officier des Arts et des Lettres, France (2000); Foundation for Art of the Canton de Vaud, for influence in art (2006); Merit Design Preis Schweiz (2007); Honorary doctorate, European University, Barcelona (2007); Prix de la Ville de Lausanne (2009); and Officier de l'Ordre des Palmes Académiques, France (2011).

But there is no retirement as Pierre Keller went on to be appointed president of OVV (Office des Vins Vaudois) which is dedicated to promote Swiss Wines from Canton Vaud worldwide. The French speaking area is well known for the production of the finest Chasselas wines. In 2013, he was in Tokyo in a joint promotion with Hublot which included a wine tasting of Canton Vaud wines.

"I live in a wine village, St Saphorin and I love Chasselas!" he said, "and I travel worldwide to promote the wines. On my schedule is Tokyo, Shanghai, St Petersburg and Rio de Janeiro."

Rivaz

Lavaux Vinorama

Route du Lac 2
CH-1071 Rivaz
Tel 021 946 3131
info@lavaux-vinorama.ch

Opening times.
June - October. From Monday - Saturday: 10.30 - 20.30. Sunday: 10.30 - 17.00
November to December and February to May. From Wednesday - Saturday: 10.30 - 20.30. Sunday: 10.30 - 17.00

For visitors who are keen to see and understand the UNESCO Lavaux vineyards, the Vinorama is unmissable for two reasons. There is a choice of over 270 local wines to taste and the movie, The Winemakers Year. It depicts the life of a winemaker throughout the year. "Each morning reveals a new mystery," said the narrator. "With each rising of the sun, I scan the sky and dutifully observe nature for my life is tied to the vagaries of the climate, to the cycles of the seasons."

The movie which is in eight languages (French, English, German, Italian, Spanish, Japanese, Mandarin and Russian) sets the scene for the Lavaux wines which are on display. The winemakers range from Lausanne to Chillon Castle and a map shows the various terroirs such as Dezaley, Calamin, Vilette and Lutry.

"I came to wine rather late because I grew up in the watchmaking area - valley de Joux," said Sandra Joye, the manager of Lavaux Vinorama. "But as I love perfume which is a cousin to wine because of the similar categories of citrus, sweetness, spicyness etc. and the smell, it was easy to appreciate them. Chasselas which is prevalent in Lavaux is a non-aromatic grape and takes on the character of the soil."

Her favourite wine comes from the Calamin terroir which has a high minerality with a bitter aftertaste. The characteristic represents the purest form of the Chasselas. The Dezaley terroir produces a more complex wine suited for gourmet dining. She is ably assisted by Tony Lewis, a wine expert and American who has gone native and even speaks schweizerdeutsch, among other languages. Various tasting packages are available including the Discovery which consists of two Chasselas and a red indigenous wine, Plant Robert, and the Expert with three Chasselas and two reds. The Aperitif plate with cheese and dried meet from the region is also available. (See entries Brotherhood of the Winegrowers festival, the Confrérie des Vignerons Museum and François Margot.)

Pierre Bise

Editions de L'Arrosoir
Chemin de Jolimont 6
1510 Moudon
Tel 021 905 3224
Mob 079 4188270
p.bise@bluewin.ch
www.pierrebise-photos.com

A special memento of a visit to the Lavaux Vineyards is a postcard or calendar by Pierre Bise. It easily can be taken as an example of art photography and can be found in shops along the Rue des deux Marchés, Vevey such as L'air du Temps.

Pierre Bise was a long distance truck driver until he retired at the age of 60 with bad knees. He had never showed any interest in photography in his life until one day he took a snap of a castle in the town Rue, Fribourg. It turned out to be so popular that he decided to become a photographer. As he had no qualifications, no one wanted to help him. So he went into business on his own as a photographer and publisher of postcards and calendars.

"I enjoy going on a walkabout and when I find an interesting view, I take a picture," he said. "I don't hang around like an angler waiting for the right moment. I just look at the weather forecast and out I go."

Rivaz

Bise's series on the landscapes of Vaud region around Lake Geneva are incredible in terms of composition. Browse the website and you will see that he has a natural talent for photography. He has without doubt a great future ahead of him. Just take the example of another long distance truck driver who succeeded in art. Jerry Saltz,also self-taught, became a top American art critic and columnist.

be undertaken to Montreux, Evian les Bain and St-Gingolph.

Cully

Cully

Cully is a cultural village with top events like the Cully Jazz Festival and Cully Classique and with the medieval buildings, make it an unmissable for tourists.

Major Davel Hotel-Restaurant

Place d'armes 8
1096 Cully
Tel 021 799 94 94
info@hotelaumajordavel.ch
www.hotelaumajordavel.ch

There are family hotels and family hotels. Some only pay lip service to the name but Bernadette and Rolf Messmer run one of the best family hotels in the Montreux Riviera. The location is unbeatable as it's right on the lake shore. The pier is a short distance away and boat trips by CGN can be undertaken to Montreux, Evian les Bain and St-Gingolph.

The rooms are pleasant if not luxurious and have superb views of Lake Geneva, the Lavaux vineyards and the Alps. Each room has a different decor and an outstanding feature is the high sleep quality. The cooking in the restaurant is excellent and the cuisine is fresh food from the market and fish from the lake - cuisine de marché. The specialities include a double (500 gm) entrecote steak with béarnaise sauce for two people and Golden trout off the bone.

"Our USP at the hotel is that we don't have a television or radio in the bedrooms," said Bernadette Messmer who is the hotel manager. "Major Davel

Bernadette and Rolf Messmer and staff

is a place to relax and to switch-off. We find that businessmen who have clients in Lausanne or Montreux are catching on. We even have a Parisian client who finds that the quietness increases his power of concentration and recharges his batteries."

Bernadette who was born in Gruyere, trained as a secretary in hospitality administration and was a flight attendant on Swissair. Her background provides her with qualities which enables her to deal with her guests' needs from advice on cultural activities, transport and excursions in the vineyards and Cully's three beaches. "I prefer to keep the dishes simple," said Rolf Messmer who is the chef." I'm proud of the high quality of the food and I never stint on the price of products. What clients also like is to have the fish deboned or the meat sliced in the front of them."

Rolf who comes from Germany across the border from Basel was an apprentice chef. He has worked in top hotels like the Swisshotels and the Euler hotel in Basel. He met Bernadette and they married in 1985. They came to Cully in 1991 and have run the Hotel-restaurant Major Davel since 1993.

"We have old fashioned values but are opened-minded to new trends," said Rolf. "If it fits with our philosophy or not." Bernadette smiles when she talks about her approach. "Just work and move yourself."

Auberge du Raisin

Place de l'Hôtel -de-Ville 1
1096 Cully
Tel 021 799 2131
info@aubergeduraisin.ch
www.aubergeduraisin.ch

An elegant Swiss inn which was built in the 16th century and blends in well with the medieval wine village. A sign of gilded grapes hangs outside while the interior surprises with its spaciousness in the staircases, bedrooms and inviting terrace on the first floor with a view of lake Geneva. It looks like a well-kept church with Burgundy stone floors, large furniture and wooden ceilings. Flowers are everywhere in casual displays to welcome the guests and look as if they have just been brought in from the garden.
The auberge is a charming 3-star hotel with 10 bedrooms, beautifully furnished with striking artworks and antique furniture. It includes two suites both with a fireplace and there is even a choice of a four-poster bed.

Fine dining includes a choice of the gourmand restaurant with a rotisserie and the bistro. Typical dishes include spicy foie gras, lobster casserole with mint coulis, veal with mushrooms and chives cream and lemongrass steak with wine sauce. There also is grilled beef and poultry as well as fresh fish from the lake.

In all, a wonderful place to stay but something you can expect from the Gauer family who have been tenants of the Auberge since 1959. They have a top reputation for luxury hospitality. Jean-Jacques runs the famous Lausanne Palace and his son, Jay, the hotel Trois Couronnes in Vevey.

Auberge de la Gare

Rue de la Gare 1
1091 Grandvaux
Tel 021 799 2686
info@aubergegrandvaux,ch
www.aubergegrandvaux

Philippe Delessert and his wife Raymonde run the restaurant and five-bedroomed 3-star auberge. The place is so popular that diners have to book in advance. Philippe is a jolly chef with a difference. He is not round and slow but lean and active.

The Auberge de la Gare is situated in the heart of the Lavaux vineyards and with a panoramic terrace. It's an idyllic spot for walkers who can be rewarded with splendid cuisine and good night's sleep after their daily exploits. The hotel is open seven days a week and to avoid disappointment with the restaurant please note it's closed on Sundays and Mondays.

3

Concerts 'OFF during family day. Wine tasting reception after concert at Potterat cellar ©Anne-Laure Lechat

Events

Cully Classique

Temple 23
CP 105
CH-1096 Cully
Tel 021 311 0229
www.cullyclassique.ch

Cully Classique had an interesting start. The cellist Marcus Hagemann came to Cully in 2003 to collect his new cello from the violin maker, Mickael Stürzenhofecker's workshop. He fell in love with the village and considered creating a music festival there. Later that year he met Jean-Christophe de Vries in Berlin and together with Albert Diringer, a piano tuner, they launched the Cully Classique Festival in 2004.

Jean-Christophe de Vries who heads the Cully Classique Festival is one of the new generation of artistic directors to watch. He is made in the same mould as one of the great impresarios of music, Martin Engstroem who established the Verbier Festival. They both have deep roots in music, are good at spotting talent and hold concerts in unlikely places. But Jean-Cristophe has an edge because he has a wider horizon than just music. He quotes the Russian composer and pianist, Alexander Scriabin's advice to Vladimir Horowitz's parents when the 11 year old played for him. "He has talent to make a really great pianist but you should give him a comprehensive cultural education."

"The aim of Cully Classique is to break the cliché that classic music is reserved only for stuffy, old people in evening wear and in an old opera house," said Jean-Christophe, director of Cully Classique. "Another objective is to destroy the wall between those who know the quality of classical music and those who don't. We began with only two concerts. An opening and a closing one. Today our classical music festival offers 100 events in 10 days. We're a unique festival because of the contrasting simplicity of the village and the highbrow concerts and artists. The whole village participates during the event. As a wine village, our concerts also take place in the cellars of winemakers. It creates an intimate atmosphere as you can meet the musicians, the staff, the audience and the inhabitants."

Jean-Christophe de Vries studied music, musicology and German literature at the Lausanne conservatory and Geneva university. He is a pianist and musicologist and comes from a musical family. Both his grandmothers were musicians and his parents played the piano, specially Bach which he hated as a child. After 25 years, he too enjoys Bach. He still likes to play for about an hour and a half each day.

"I was a volunteer at the Verbier Festival for eight years," he said, "It's a top international classical music event and I was able to judge the positive and negative aspects. What I disliked the exclusivity such as the private parties in the chalets. It separated the artists from the audience and the locals. But the Verbier Festival academy was magical because it identifies, encourages and nurtures tomorrow's exceptional musical talent."

"At the Cully Classique, we've had several breakthroughs," he continued. "In 2006, the locals opened their houses to the musicians and offered free accommodation. They were welcomed for 500 nights within ten days. It was a great idea because it shattered the stereotype in the local's minds that musicians were an old, grumpy and boring bunch of people. Indeed, when they saw how glamorous the young musicians like the soprano, Bettina Gfeller, and the pianist Juliette Granier Calva were, they were knocked over.

"Then when they experienced such joyous performances from the gipsy group, Taraf de Haïdouks, everybody wanted them to stay. Another breakthrough was the free concerts which were introduced in 2010 and attracted a lot of locals and people from the region. They had an opportunity to experience concerts and as they liked them, we had a new audience."

Cully Classique consists of two types of concerts. The Festival'In offers an original programme as well as music structured around an annual theme. Last year, it was the spirituality of music and included gipsy, Indian and Jewish music. The Festival'Off offers free concerts and other activities. There some 12 venues including the two churches which both have good acoustics, the wine cellars of Potterat and the Caveau de Vignerons where 14 of winemakers present their wine, the 17th century old wine press room, the modern Davel hall and the violin workshop of Mickael Stürzenhofecker, among others. Cully Classique also has an academic programme for young musicians called Vis- à-vis. Advanced students from European conservatories are brought together with internationally renowned musicians in Cully for public rehearsals and concerts.

"My philosophy is based on contrasts," he said. "There's the analogy of the church and its carnival. We have the same with the serious concerts followed by fun afterwards. Then there's the simple life in the village and the grandeur of the scenery. Classical music is like oxygen for me but it's not enough. I need to dip into the rich source of culture."

In 2014, among the discoveries were Olivia Gay, a French cellist and Natacha Kudritskaya a Ukrainian pianist. They played to three encores and gave a brilliant performances. Natacha's playing was full of emotion and she seemed to dance before the piano with her head and hands.

Cully Jazz Festival

Place de l'Hotel-de-Ville 2
CP138
1096 Cully
Tel 021 799 9900
info@cullyjazz.ch
www.cullyjazz.ch

The Cully Jazz festival is the other festival in the Montreux Riviera, the more intimate and human-sized one. For more than 30 years, it has been offering free and paid concerts in several locations such as the big hall, 13 cafes and wine cellars. It has been held for over 30 years and was founded by Daniel Thentz, a trumpet player and Emmanuel Gétaz, two locals from Cully.

Cully Jazz festival

“People often think that we compete with our big brother the Montreux Jazz Fesitval,” said Benoît Frund who is the festival’s president. “But they’re mistaken. Montreux’s a city and we’re in the middle of the vineyards. We’re very localised and it’s easy to meet villagers. We never use big screens and the audience is always near the artists. We attract about 50,000 people over nine days whereas Montreux Jazz Festival which is the second largest in the world has audiences of over 200,000.”

Benoît Frund who is a Vice Rector of sustainability and the campus at the University of Lausanne is one of several volunteers who runs the festival. He was born in Riex which is near Cully and was asked by friends to help some 18 years ago. He is proud that except for a couple of administrators who are paid, the rest of the committee are volunteers.

“It’s very democratic,” he said. “We work together and decide everything together.” The volunteers include Jean-Yves Cavin, the two Potterat brothers, Nicolas and Guillaume who live in Cully and Carine Zuber who runs the Moods Jazz club in Zurich, among others.

“What I like about jazz,” said Carine, “is that you never know what to expect. Jazz is per concert music.”

Winemakers

Cave de Moratel

Family Longet-Voruz
Route de vevey 49
1096 Cully
Tel 079 6454066
www.cavedemoratel.ch

The Longets have worked their vineyards for three generations. It was begun by Patricia Longet-Voruz's grandfather, Henri, and after her father retired, she and her husband, Denis took over. The small vineyard of two hectares is conveniently situated around their home which was built in 1560 and in two km away. This enables the couple to work it themselves without seasonal workers.

"We're ecological and produce our wines according to the standards of Vinatura," said Patricia who is a charming and modest woman. "An added benefit is that we don't use machines in the vineyard as we do everything by hand. We walk there and I'm proud because we monitor our wine right up to the sale. At the end of winter, we prune the branches which are used as fertiliser and in between often visit the vineyards to take care of the grapes. Later in the autumn we harvest the grapes. The only duties we do separately is the vinification which Denis likes to do on his own and the accounts which are my responsibility.

The wine cellar has a unique wine tasting room as well a carnozet for a group of people. The range of wines is small but select and include three reds - a Merlot, Pinot Noir and Diolinoir and two whites - Chasselas and Viognier. The arty labels on the bottles were designed by Patricia and a tour of the wine cellar as well as the vineyards can be arranged.

"The most popular is our award-winning white, Les Blonnaises," from the famous domaine of Epesses, "she said. "The Diolinoir which was created by crossing two different red grapes and is liked by visitors because of the unusual grape variety."

A visit to the Family Longet-Voruz is recommended because of the ambiance and the warm welcome given. A guest room is also available and an overnight stay enables visitors to enjoy the cultural village of Cully. The good news is that you're never to far from Longet- Voruz wines as all the restaurants stock them.

Lutry

Lutry is a small medieval town on the shores of lake Geneva. It is well preserved with narrow streets and numerous merchants' and noblemens' houses from 15th to 18th centuries. There is a marked circular walk with eleven information boards about the history of Lutry. The town as well as the two hamlets Châtelard and Savuit are part of the Swiss Heritage Sites.

"The population has grown steadily over the years and we have a total of 9,500," said Jacques-Andre Conne the mayor of Lutry, "which means that we are close to a city status once 10,000 is reached. We have an active local economy including wineries, craftsmen, shopkeepers, restaurant owners, services and some farmers as well as 500 small and medium sized firms. In the 1960s, we became part of greater Lausanne and became a popular area for the wealthy sector. Some 27% of the population are foreigners, among them about 200 are British."

Lutry vineyards covers 130 hectares and are part of the UNESCO Lavaux vineyards. There are 27 wineries in the town and an annual harvest wine festival is held over three days in late September. All the wine cellars are open to the public and a highlight is the famous parade of some 600 children on the Sunday.

"There's an old saying about our wine," said Jacques-Andre Conne. "When you drink Lutry's wine, it doesn't slake the thirst, it increases it. The town has three hectares and produces Chasselas and Pinot Noir at our property at Châtelard. I advise visitors to take the little train, the Lavaux Express, on a round trip to Grandvaux. From April to October the train which operates from our landing pier, enables people to discover the breathtaking terraced vineyards which were cultivated by generations of Lutry inhabitants. Viticulture was initiated by the Benedictine monks between the 11th and 12th century."

Lutry has several attractions during the year like ice skating in the winter and swimming in the summer at a splendid natural beach. Cultural events include the JS Bach concerts and organ recitals. There is Lutry castle dating from the 15th to 16th centuries and St Martin church which was built on the foundation of a Romanesque church.

"One of the problems, we have solved is accommodation," he said. "Once a town becomes popular, the price of construction increases and homes become unaffordable for young generation. We have built more than 30 apartments on a cooperative basis to reduce costs, provided low land prices and involved no developers or estate agents. Another future project is education. At present, some of our children attend school in Pully but as the numbers of students increase we have a project to build a new school in Lutry."

3

Timeless Bach

JS Bach concerts have been organised in the Lutry church for over a half century. It was founded by the oboist Edgar Shann in 1957. The concerts have been characterised by a chronic lack of money and surrounded by friends and volunteers always ready to help. The then little known Karl Richter was offered a Omega watch as a fee and the podium was cobbled together in the church by the carpenter Aviolat Grandvaux.

Today, the artistic director is Bernadette Elöd a violinist who fled Hungary after the revolution. She was a pupil of the violinist Arpàd Gérecz who was the second artistic director of the Bach concerts. The programme runs from November to April and every second year, there is the 'Crazy Bach Days' in May during which an exhibition of documents and programmes is held in the Castle.

"The past 30 years of Bach concerts have been a joyous participation of a rich musical heritage," said Bernadette Elöd. "I have measured out my life with intense meetings with artists. I'll never forget when Yehudi Menuhin entered the church and the audience gasped and rose to their feet spontaneously. During the interval, we met in a room which had a large table with a vase of lilacs in the middle. He was a small man and had to stand on tiptoe to smell the scent.

"Another encounter was with András Schiff who opened up half of heaven with the Goldberg variations. After he played the 30 variations, it is customary to start with the first again. But at the end, some people began to applaud and he received a standing ovation. Then he played the first variation and he received a second standing ovation. As an encore he played the 1st sonata of Beethoven - a whole 20 minutes! He was great stickler for silence during his performances. Once a woman coughed and he stopped playing. 'Will someone give that woman a sweet to suck,' was his retort.

The acoustics in Lutry church are excellent and over the years audiences have been treated to many performances by top musicians, choirs and ensembles. For example, Ton Koopman with the Amsterdam Barock Orchestra; Sigiswald Kuijken with the La Petite Bande; Il Giardino Armonico; Franz Liszt Chamber Orchestra Budapest; Kammerorchester Basel with the famous trumpet player, Sergei Nakariakov; two Hungarian artists, Jànos Starker, cellist and György Sebök, pianist, among many others.

Anne-Caroline Prénat at the organ

Lutry Organ and Organist

Anne-Caroline Prénat who lives in Belmont-sur-Lausanne is a top organist at the Lutry church for over 20 years.

The organ which was inaugurated in 1791 was built by a famous French organ builder, Jean-Jacques Zimmer. The whole instrument was enlarged and restored in 1913 and again in 1975 by Hans Füglister from Grimisuat (near Sion)1975. There are 39 registers distributed on three keyboards and the pedal keyboard.

Lutry Church

The Reformed Church of Saint-Martin was built on the foundation of an earlier Romanesque priory church of the Benedictines in the 11th century. The current church was built in multiple stages. The polygonal choir built in 1260 is the oldest part. It is vaulted with gothic arches and has a liturgical basin in the south wall. The painted ceiling which is a rare masterpiece was created by Humbert Maresche after the Reformation.

The Bernese offered the church to the parishioners who had converted from Catholicism to Protestantism. In former times, it consisted of two parts which was symbolised by the colour yellow the parishioners in the nave and russet for the months in the choir stalls.

Vincent Tearoom

22 Grand-Rue
Tel 021 791 1982
www.patisserie-vincent.ch

Open from 6.30 am to 6.30 pm on weekdays. On Saturday and Sunday from 7 am to 6 pm. Closed Mondays and January 1.

Lucien Moutarlier

Grand-Rue 1, 1095
Lutry, Switzerland
021 791 59 80
www.moutarlier.ch

Superb quality products. He provides excellent range of lunch snacks, real French croissant and delicious mouth-watering chocolates and patisserie.

Lucien Moutarlier who was born in Nantes, France now lives with his family in Chexbres. He is a patisseur, confiseur and traiteur with shops in Lutry, Lausanne, Chexbres and Montreux. His two sons, Damien who is a patisseur and Christophe, a chocolatier, work with him.

Lucien Moutarlier

Chapter 4. La Tour de Peilz

History and People

Lyonel Kaufmann is the mayor of La Tour de Peilz, a small town wedged between Montreux and Vevey. Its history is bound to the castle which was given to the town by the Count of Savoy in 1282. The castle is represented on the coat of arms and today has been turned into a Swiss Museum of Games. Like other cities in Switzerland, La Tour de Peilz has a twin in France - Ornans. There is a special reason for this is as the painter Gustave Courbet who was born in Ornans, spent the last years of his life there. He was an innovator who led the Realist movement in 19th century painting in France.

"We have a statue outside the Commune sculpted by Courbet," said Kaufmann.

Lyonel Kaufmann, Mayor of Tour de Peilz with Courbet's bust of Helvetia ©Christophe Karlen

"It's called Liberty and is a bust of a beautiful woman. In France such a bust is called Marianne and is the national emblem, a portrayal of the Goddess of Liberty. Courbet first called it Helvetia and put the Swiss flag on it. However, the Municipality found those items political and he was asked to replace it by a more neutral symbol. Courbet agreed and put a star on the statue's chest. The statue was a gift but the plinth cost the commune 500 francs. Money, he badly needed to pay off a debt in France."

The statue was inaugurated on August 15, 1875 with the inscription on the plinth: Thank you for the hospitality. Courbet made 10 plaster casts to give to other Cantons and cities like Martigny. The model for the bust is unknown. It is thought either to be Mme Arnaud de l'Ariege from Clarens or a young woman from Pontarlier who helped him to escape from France.

Courbet had fled to Switzerland in 1874 after he had been fined 323,019 francs 68 centimes for toppling the Vendôme Column in 1871. A French court ruled that he could pay the fine in instalments for 33 years until his 91st birthday. Courbet lived in Bon-Port and was a habitué of the Cafe du Centre which was demolished in the 1980s. The last owner still has the table where he used to drink. He died, aged 58, of a liver disease aggravated by heavy drinking.

"Today, we have other well known inhabitants," he said. "The first Swiss astronaut Claude Nicollier who had flown on four Space Shuttle missions and Claude de Ribaupierre who is a Swiss francophone comics creator, one of the most famous in Europe and known as Derib. Of course, there is also Jean-Claude Biver, the famous watch innovator who has a farm and makes his own cheese. "

Kaufmann has had a varied career before he entered politics. He first gained a diploma in business studies in 1985 while he worked for the Winterthur Insurance company. His next move was to study history, French and economics at the University of Lausanne in 1991 and where he finally obtained a Doctor of Letters in 2013. Further work experience was gained as a teacher at the colleges Bethusy in Lausanne and Oron-la-Ville.

"Of the residents, 28% are foreign nationals," said Kaufmann. "The age of the population is more or less evenly distributed between the young, the middle aged and the elderly. La Tour de Peilz is a net exporter of workers - a commuter town, as about three workers leave every day compared to one entering it."

The Swiss museum of games
Musée Suisse du Jeu

1814 La Tour de Peilz
Tel 021 9772300
info@museedujeu.com
www.museedujeu.com

The museum is located in a historic castle which Peter II of Savoy built in the 13th century. The unusual museum which is on the upper two floors covers the history of games throughout the world and includes various types such as strategy, risk, memory, role- playing, education etc. The exhibition varies from games-in-the-sand from Africa to sophisticated video games and gambling equipment. A few games are set aside for children and a special teaching box is available at reception. The director is Ulrich Schädler, a world expert on games.

Visitors can climb the tower of the castle and enjoy the view at the top. To the east the Dents du Midi and to the west the Lavaux vineyards.

La Tour de Peilz is the headquarters of Nestlé Switzerland and Atlanship SA, a shipping company specializing in the transport of orange juice in its fleet of refrigerated tanker ships. The American Graduate School of Business (AGSB) is also located in the city.

Over the years it has attracted all sorts of people including A.J.Cronin who was buried there; The son of Kaiser Willem II, Prince Adalbert of Prussia and his wife, Princess Adelheid of Saxe-Meiningen; Jacques Piccard, oceanographer who died there; Shania Twain, a Canadian country, pop singer and songwriter; Thomas Zoells, founder of PianoForte Foundation, Chicago; Dimitry Markevitch, the cellist who was born there; and tennis player Manuela Maleeva-Fragniere and her family.

La Tour de Peilz also has Villa Kenwin which is a listed building by the Swiss National Heritage. It was built in 1930-1931 by Hermann Henselmann for Kenneth Macpherson and Winifred Ellerman (Bryher) who lived there with their American friend the poet H.D. (Hilda Doolittle-Aldington) and her daughter Perdita.

The last word on such an interesting place should be given to Courbet. "I am fifty years old and I have always lived in freedom; let me end my life free; when I am dead let this be said of me: 'He belonged to no school, to no church, to no institution, to no academy, least of all to any régime except the régime of liberty.'"

Chapter 5. Villeneuve

History

Patricia Dominique Lachat is one of the few female mayors in the Montreux Riviera. Her municipality is the tranquil village of Villeneuve which celebrated its 800th anniversary in 2014 and was founded by Count Thomas of Savoy. It is located at the beginning of lake Geneva at the foot of Mt Arvel and Rochers-de-Naye and on their slopes are forests and terraces of vineyards. It adjoins Grangettes, a nature reserve, which is a paradise for 260 species of birds with reed beds, marshes and ponds. At the outskirts of the village is a commercial centre with several supermarkets and stores.

Patricia Dominique Lachat, Mayor of Villeneuve

"In 2011, I was asked out of the blue to join the municipality," she said, " and I thought why not? I live in the village, my children have gone to school here and I like Villeneuve and the area. It would be good to be able to make contribution as a way of thanks. So I was elected on the council in 2006 as a socialist. My portfolios were police, security and policing unauthorised constructions. I made an effort to learn more about both areas as I don't want to be token woman on the council. So I went on a course at the Swiss Institute of Police. It was a tough experience with the policemen because of two impediments: I was a socialist who is supposed to be soft and a woman. But I ended up with policemen's respect because I was a sharpshooter with a pistol. At one time, I even gave lessons at a shooting range."

5

In 2011, to her surprise, she was elected mayor. She is trilingual and speaks, French, German and Italian, and has a good knowledge of English. Such skills enable her to identify with national and regional issues. Her main platform for the election was social achievements, fair and equitable tax revenues and an effective public service.

In addition to her work as mayor where the emphasis is on administration, she is a MP for the Canton Vaud which she enjoys because there is an opportunity to legislate among other things. She is also president of both the Business and Professional Women Club (BPW), Lausanne and of the Swiss aesthetician owners association as well as a committee member of the organisation for professional retraining (OSEO).

Naturally, Dominique Lachat would expect tourists to be open-minded when they visit Villeneuve. They will discover the following: it was a lakeside Roman town called Pennelucos (head of the lake); there are 14 winemakers including vins des hospices cantonal, the association viticole, Cave Bertolet, Cave des Rois, among others; there are two fisherman and fresh fish can be bought including tartare fera; there are 11 walks around the Montreux Riviera including a nature hike to Grangettes and Le Bouveret (and return by boat) and others through the natural park Gruyère Pays-d'Enhaut; the special hard cheese, l'Etival made from unpasteurised milk when cows graze on the Alpine meadows during the summer; a visit to the small Romanesque church and the attractive municipal hall which was a former hospice chapel.

Strangers are our Friends

Luciano and Verena Lepre have lived in Villeneuve for over 34 years. They have a dog called Shiraz and outwardly they blend in with the other villagers. But the couple have had remarkable lives. They cycled around the world for eight years on bicycles. A truly amazing feat!

"We quit our jobs and cycled east in the general direction of Kathmandu, Nepal, where we had friends," they said. "We had no definite plans, no set route and no itinerary. It was total freedom. The trip transformed us and made us feel a warm and awesome respect for this earth. Each day we looked forward to a new adventure, wondering who we would meet and which way we would cycle. Perhaps at the end of the day, we would have made new friends or had a meaningful conversation or just shared a smile. Despite the uncertainty, we were certain that the unknown could be an opportunity and the stranger could become a friend."

Luciano who comes from the Dolomites met Verena in Davos at the staff swimming pool of a hospital. Verena worked as a nurse and Luciano who trained as a sociologist was a sales rep for a pharmaceutical company. Luciano was instantly attracted by Verena in her swimming costume and they married in 1976. A friend told them about Villeneuve and they came to the village in 1980. They found a house similar to Verena's flat in Davos and bought it.

"As a boy, I was always fascinated by travel, " said Luciano. "I read the Travels of Marco Polo and other books about travellers. It was not easy to travel some 30 years ago and there was no Lonely Planet guide."

Before they took off on their bicycles on September 4, 1996, they had experience of backpacking on two trips around the world. This had whet their appetite and as they were entering their forties, they resigned their jobs - Verena as sales rep for a pharmaceutical company and Luciano as a sales rep for household electronics and mobile phones. They pedalled their way to the Middle East and entered Asia and made their way to Australia via Japan and the Americas before they returned to Europe. They rode between four to six hours a day and visited some 42 countries in all. The bicycles were donated by Lidia Lepre, Luciano's mother.

"It was a trip undertaken with no sponsors otherwise our freedom would have been limited," said Luciano, "and we rode on simple cycles loaded with a 4 m2 non-waterproof tent, a portable stove and cooking utensils. We deliberately didn't opt for high-tech equipment as we wanted to meet people on a basic level without stirring any envy. On hindsight, it was a good policy as we could ask strangers whether we could put up our tent in their garden or question them about a route or the weather. We had a limited budget of about CHF 10 a day and where we could, we earned money by selling our stories to magazines. I took up photography by necessity."

It took them 14 months to reach Nepal where they stayed for four months with their friends. The highlight of their trip was the year in Japan. They were frequently asked by people to spend the night in ordinary homes.

"One of the things we found on the trip is that you can be happy with a few things in life," they said. "You can discover yourself

Verena and Luciano Lepre at Wadi Rum, Jordan ©Veraluc photography

in travel. To quote Nicolas Bouvier, the Swiss traveller and writer, 'you think that you're going to make a journey yet soon the journey makes or unmakes you.'"

"My most memorable experience of the trip," said Verena," was when I once collapsed from the heat in Turkey. I was revived when someone put lemon drops on my tongue. My eyes opened and I just saw this dark man above me. I never got a chance to thank him. It confirmed for me that every stranger can become a friend. Looking back, it was a miracle that we managed to stay safe."

After such a mind-boggling experience, one may ask how they settled down to a normal life. Verena works in a hospice and tends to terminally ill patients. She also is volunteer in the community to help immigrants.

Durgnat

Grand Rue 2
1844 Villneuve
Tel 021 9681275
www.durgnat.info
Open from Tuesday to Sunday morning from 6 am to 6.30 pm

Durgnat 'La Boutique'

Grand Rue 61
1844 Villneuve
Tel 021 9601076
Open from Wednesday to Sunday from 6 am to 6.30 pm

Fabienne Durgnat is the third generation to run the boulangerie/patisserie/confiserie tearoom in Villeneuve. She's a slim woman and if you looked at her, you wouldn't dream that any chocolates or pastries passed her lips. But the contrary is true. She like her regular customers have no popular tastes - they enjoy everything on offer.

One of the unusual cakes that catches the eye in the display is the 'religieuse' because of its double pastry case. On top the egg white patisserie and below almond cream. It's known as the nun because it represents a nun in a habit. But few will know of its Italian origin. It was made for the Queen of France, Catherine de Medici, who was the wife of King Henri II.

"When I took over the business from my parents, Michel and Therese," she said, "I kept some of the patisserie from my grandfather's time like the 'religieuse' and the Villeneuve cake from my father's time. The rest is new and is changed every month and seasonally. Sometimes we use vegetables such as courgettes, tomato and carrots in our patisserie. But everything in the tearoom is handmade. All we do is to buy the ingredients. That's the tradition started by my grandparents, René and Ruth, when they opened Durgnat in 1951."

Fabienne did her apprenticeship as a patisseur/confiserie in Aigle. When she gained her diploma she worked in various top establishments in the Valais such as Taillens, Crans- Montana and in Vaud like Artifoni in Corsier, Hedinger in Aigle and Lucien Moutarlier, Chexbres. With such experience behind her, she was ready to work for the family business.

"It meant waking up at 4 am to make the different patisserie for the day," she said. "My husband, Cyrille was a chef and did a second apprenticeship as patisseur/confiserie. He is the baker and gets up at 1am to bake the range of breads. My inspiration for patisserie and confiserie comes when we go on walks. The changes in the seasonal colours stimulate me to think of new products."

Besides the coffee and teas served, Durgnat also offers lunch of fresh salads including the Caesar salad with grilled chicken, soups, omeletes, sandwiches and quiches at Grand Rue 2 and another selection at La Boutique with crepes and hot paninis as well as salads. The workroom for the patisserie and artistic

Fabienne Durgnat

creations made for celebrations and festivals is at the other end of Rue Grand at 61.

"I encourage school groups to visit our workroom," she said. "They are amazed at what we do. And I'm proud that when they return home they tell their parents. It's good for the village to know that we do everything ourselves."

The specialities in the range of products include the Durgnat Panetone, the Mozart truffles, their homemade ice cream in unusual flavours like vanilla/apricot/ meringue or tart/citron/ crumble and their kilo bread which is half white, 45 cm long and weighs a kilo. It's good for picnics and families. The fact that the tearoom is patronised by 90% of the locals is proof of the high quality of the products and the friendly service

Index